CHRISTIAN PRIESTHOOD EXAMINED

CHRISTIAN PRIESTHOOD EXAMINED

by

RICHARD HANSON

Professor of Historical and Contemporary Theology
University of Manchester

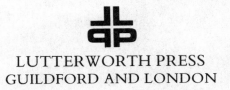

LUTTERWORTH PRESS
GUILDFORD AND LONDON

First published 1979

This book is dedicated to
FREDERICK FYVIE BRUCE D.D., F.B.A.
formerly a colleague in the
Faculty of Theology
of the University of Manchester

PIGNUS AMICITIAE

ISBN 0 7188 2400 8

*Filmset in 11/12 point Bembo
Printed and bound in Great Britain
by W & J Mackay Limited, Chatham*

CONTENTS

1

EVIDENCE IN THE NEW TESTAMENT

Priesthood: an Uncertain Term

The word 'priest' arouses very different sentiments in different people. For some the word produces instant hostility. It is associated with priestcraft and priestly powers, with a powerful caste within the church exercising irresponsible authority through the confessional and the pulpit. It suggests a system whereby God can only be approached through the members of this caste who have exclusive control of the means of grace and who use this control to overawe and delude their docile flock. It suggests someone who interferes, intervenes, between man and God. We can think of the cardinals in Shakespeare's *King John* and Webster's *Duchess of Malfi*. To others the word 'priest' has a glad and comforting sound. It suggests a champion, a comforter, a support for the uncertain or oppressed or needy laity, someone who sacrifices himself for his people, who devotes his life to caring for them and serving them. We can recall the lines of the poet Mangan:

> O, my dark Rosaleen,
>> Do not sigh, do not weep . . .
> The priests are on the ocean green,
>> They march along the deep.

Others, again, do not respond to the word with such strong feelings in either direction, but recall that almost all religions have in some form or other produced priests and do not therefore find it extraordinary that the Christian religion should have priests, but reasonably enough expect those who use the word to have clear ideas about what they mean by priest and priesthood.

When we speak of Christian priesthood, however, it is not

7

easy to find clear ideas whereby to define the terms associated with the concept. It is not a subject which has attracted much scholarly attention in recent years, even though three major denominations, the Roman Catholic, the Orthodox and the Anglican, formally use the term to denote the majority of their clergy and continue to ordain new priests every year. The reasons for the neglect and confusion which have recently attended this subject are clear enough. Until recently those denominations which ordain priests believed and claimed that Jesus Christ, or at least his apostles, ordained priests at the very beginning, and those denominations which do not ordain priests denied this belief and claim. The first group therefore thought that there was nothing to explain about the origin of a Christian priesthood, and the second thought that there was nothing to discuss; priesthood did not belong to the original ministry of the church, whereas other forms of ministry existing in the church today had so belonged.

If the assumptions upon which both points of view have long rested are destroyed, as this book is intended to destroy them, then it is obvious that we are faced with a new situation in which the whole question of Christian priesthood becomes uncertain and must be examined *de novo*. It is curious that neither those who favour a Christian priesthood nor those who reject it have been concerned to examine the evidence. This book is written in the belief that it is now possible, once traditional and conventional ideas about both ministry and priesthood have been abandoned, to see with reasonable clarity why, how and when a Christian priesthood arose and to assess its authenticity.

No Ministers in the Primitive Church

As we approach the subject of Christian priesthood, it is first necessary to face the question of Christian ministry generally. When we speak today of Christian ministers and the Christian ministry we invariably mean ministry as the great majority of Christian denominations know it today, that is a ministry consisting of officers appointed to fill official posts in the church who have themselves succeeded to officers filling these

8

posts before them and who will in course of time be succeeded by other officers who will fill their posts when they retire or leave or die. This concept of ministry, which I shall call 'official ministry' is usually applied to full-time permanent ministers, but it can also be applied to part-time ministers and even to those who occupy a ministry for a defined period and then leave it. The essential point about this type of ministry is that it consists of an office to be filled, to which officials can succeed; also that it is either permanent or for a determined time, not occasional or *ad hoc*. This definition of ministry applies to almost all forms of ministry filled by Christian ministers today, whether they are popes or archbishops or bishops or priests or deacons or pastors or just ministers, whether they claim apostolic succession or scriptural authority or not, whether they are paid or unpaid, established or free, male or female, whether they wear clerical collars or do not, whether they call themselves Catholic or Reformed, apostolic or evangelical.

It must first be understood that in the earliest age of the church no such ministry as this existed, and therefore that no such ministry, in any of its forms, can justly claim that it was instituted by Christ or his apostles, nor that it has any particular right to call itself exclusively scriptural. This statement when it is first heard usually arouses astonishment and incredulity in its hearers. So entirely inured are we to assuming that ministry can mean nothing else than this ministry, that it comes to us as a shock to hear that ministry of this sort, wide as its varieties are, did not exist in the primitive church and was not of dominical or apostolic institution. Did not Jesus appoint apostles who were bishops or priests or both, or at least were ministers in our sense, and at any rate did not the apostles appoint successors in the form of bishops or priests or just ministers, presbyters or deacons? Or did not, at the very least, apostles, and especially the apostle Paul, see to it that ministers were appointed in the churches which he founded, even if we need not insist that these ministers were formally successors of Paul? Did not Jesus appoint clergy for his church when he founded it? Were there not always ministers of the gospel in our modern sense?

In order to establish the truth of the drastic statement that

9

neither Christ nor his apostles founded an official ministry we must first distinguish between the foundation of the church and the foundation of the ministry. That Christ in some sense founded a church it would be idle to deny. It is most unlikely that he called it a church, that is, that he called it by an Aramaic name of which the Greek word *ecclesia* is a translation; this fact in itself casts doubt upon the entire authenticity of the two passages Matthew 16:18 and 18:17 which are usually the two most invoked in order to prove that Jesus founded a church. But clearly Jesus chose twelve apostles and attracted to himself a band of followers, male and female, and this body constituted the continuity between the disciples of the days of the ministry of Jesus in Galilee and Jerusalem and the church of the earliest days of Christianity.

In one sense, the church sprang out of the resurrection of Jesus, and it is this aspect of the church which Paul emphasizes most strongly. He is not interested in the church as an institution founded by Christ in the days of his flesh, but only in the church as those who live in the Spirit and belong to the body of the risen Christ. But even Paul admits an indebtedness to those who were in Christ before him, to 'the apostles before me' (Gal. 1:17), and thereby implicitly allows that there was a group of people who constituted the church which continued from the days of Christ's earthly life to the days of his risen or heavenly life.

However, we must not lightly assume that references to this church in the New Testament are references to its ministry. In the earliest days the apostles are the church. When in the closing verses of Matthew's gospel Jesus gives his parting blessing and commission, he is not conferring these upon the church's ministers but upon the church. When in John 20 Jesus breathes upon the disciples (and they are carefully not called apostles but disciples) and confers on them the power of forgiving or retaining sins, this power is conferred upon the whole church, not upon the ministry as such. As we shall see, in the early days of Christianity Christians acted as if the whole church, and not merely the ministers, possessed authority. Our tendency, formed by eighteen centuries of the existence of an official ministry, is to assume that on such occasions Jesus is represented as commissioning a ministry, but we have no

10

right to make such an assumption. Christ did indeed gather a community of disciples during his earthly ministry, and this community, endowed with the Holy Spirit, became the primitive Christian church. But to recognize this is not to concede that he instituted an official ministry.

But were not the apostles, the twelve or the eleven, an official ministry? It is certainly true that the apostles take the lead in exhorting and organizing the nascent Christian community described in the book of Acts, or rather, a small inner band of them does, Peter, James and John. And among the apostolic band Peter is, at any rate at the beginning, marked out as the first, the leader. All the lists of apostles in the gospels place him first and both Paul (1 Cor. 15:5) and Mark (14:28;16:7) and perhaps Luke (23:34) recognize him as the one to whom Jesus first showed himself after the resurrection. Acts represents him as taking the initiative more than any other in the earliest days of the church. But, in the first place, we know nothing except their names about the great majority of the twelve, unless we are to accept the distribution of conversation among them by the fourth evangelist as representing a literal reporter's account. If the majority of the apostles behaved as official ministers we have no record of the fact. And conversely, James, the brother of the Lord, behaves like one of the twelve without being one. Jesus appears to him after the resurrection (1 Cor. 15:7) Paul counts him in Galatians as one of the original bearers of tradition (1:19; 2:9,12); and it is clear from the second half of Acts that by about 50 AD he was the authoritative person in the church in Jerusalem (12:17; 15:13ff; 21:18ff).

Finally, and most significantly, none of the apostles appoint successors; this essential ingredient of a ministerial office is lacking in their case. The fact is that the twelve are regarded in the New Testament as possessing a function in which there can be no successors. They are the original witnesses, those who had accompanied Jesus himself and who knew what he was like and what he had said and done. This is what they have to pass on; this is what constitutes their nature as the twelve apostles; they are the initiators of the gospel, and only they can be the first planters of it. Others later act as apostles in that they sow the seed of the good news in virgin soil, they are the first

11

to plant the church in Rome or in Ephesus or in Corinth, and in that sense they can be called apostles. But the function of the twelve cannot be repeated.

In short the apostles of Jesus will not fit into the category of ministers, of officers of the church in our modern sense. To read back into the earliest period the existence of one or more ministerial offices, and to identify the apostles with bishops or priests, or to imagine that they instituted ministers of religion as we know them is to commit a grave historical error. This anachronism was of course committed again and again in later ages, starting with the seekers after apostolic succession in the second half of the 2nd century and continuing up to our own day. But continuous repetition through the ages has not made it any less of an anachronism.

No Clergy in Paul's Letters

In handling the subject of ministry in the New Testament it is essential to remember the order in which the books of the New Testament were written. If we assume, as the order in which the books of the New Testament are now presented would lead us to assume, that the gospels were written first, and then Acts and then the letters of Paul, beginning with Romans and ending with the Pastoral Epistles to Timothy, to Titus and the Letter to Philemon, we shall never be able to understand the development of the institutions and the thought of the early church. We shall have to assume that the doctrine of Christ as the pre-existent Logos or Word was achieved before the picture of him as the Messiah, translating us into the kingdom of god and bringing in the final age to supersede this present evil age, and that Paul showed no interest at all in ministerial office when he wrote to the Corinthians and Romans, indeed held a concept of ministry which left no room for it, while at the same time he was writing to his friends in various parts of the world letters which were largely concerned with setting up just such a ministry.

But we must follow the more rational and scholarly method of accepting the results of historical criticism and find in consequence a very different picture. The earliest documents

12

of the New Testament are the letters of Paul, and these letters do not include the letters to Timothy and to Titus which on evidence of vocabulary, style and content we must conclude to have been written by somebody else who used the name of Paul and who wrote long after Paul's day, perhaps in the 2nd century. If we wish to come as close as possible to the life and thought of the primitive church, we must take as our primary documents the authentic letters of Paul. And when we question them about the form of ministry and the assumptions about ministry which existed in his day and in the churches which he founded and to which he wrote, we discover that he does not recognize the existence of anything that we should call ministerial office.

There are two passages in his letters where Paul develops his doctrine of ministry at some length—1 Corinthians 12 and Romans 12. In 1 Corinthians he is speaking of spiritual gifts, and he tries to make the Corinthians understand that gifts of this sort are not something to boast about, not something to enhance the status or feed the pride of the individual possessor of them. In the course of bringing this lesson home to his hearers Paul has occasion to say (12:4–11):

> Now there are varieties of gifts, but the same Spirit; and there are varieties of service, but the same Lord; and there are varieties of working, but it is the same God who inspires them all in every one. To each is given the manifestation of the Spirit for the common good. To one is given through the Spirit the utterance of wisdom, and to another the utterance of knowledge according to the same Spirit, to another faith by the same Spirit, to another gifts of healing by the same Spirit, to another the working of miracles, to another prophecy, to another the ability to distinguish between spirits, to another various kinds of tongues, to another the interpretation of tongues. All these are inspired by one and the same Spirit, who apportions to each one individually as he wills.

Paul in the immediately following verses then goes on to develop his famous image of Christians as the body of Christ, each member contributing his part for the benefit of the whole and himself sustained by the sympathy and common experience of the whole. He then says (vv. 27–31):

13

Now you are the body of Christ and individually members of it. And God has appointed in the church first apostles, second prophets, third teachers, then workers of miracles, then healers, helpers, administrators, speakers in various kinds of tongues. Are all apostles? Are all prophets? Are all teachers? Do all work miracles? Do all possess gifts of healing? Do all speak with tongues? Do all interpret? But earnestly desire the higher gifts.

If we try to interpret these two lists of ministries as lists of official ministries, the second offers some little hope, for it starts off with apostles, prophets and teachers in an order which might be hierarchical, even though it is difficult to envisage miracle workers, healers, those who speak in tongues and those who interpret what they are saying as official ministries. The earlier list, however, is very difficult to interpret in this way. How can we imagine the possession of a word of wisdom or the utterance of knowledge, and how can we possibly imagine the exercise of faith, as an official ministry?

The second passage, in Romans 12, is also placed in the context of an exhortation to humility and mutual concern. It runs thus (vv. 3–8):

For by the grace given to me I bid every one among you not to think of himself more highly than he ought to think, but to think with sober judgment, each according to the measure of faith which God has assigned him. For as in one body we have many members, and all the members do not have the same function, so we, though many, are one body in Christ, and individually members one of another. Having gifts that differ according to the grace that is given to us, let us use them: if prophecy, in proportion to our faith; if service, in our serving; he who teaches, in his teaching; he who exhorts, in his exhortation; he who contributes, in liberality; he who gives aid, with zeal; he who does acts of mercy, with cheerfulness.

And Paul goes on in the next few verses to speak of brotherly love, as in 1 Corinthians he followed his words about ministry with the hymn of love in chapter 13. It is to be noticed that this passage in Romans corresponds also to the passage in 1 Corinthians in connecting ministry closely with the doctrine of the church as the body of Christ, and also that Paul apparently expects the activites of each Christian in his ministry to depend upon his faith, just as he listed faith in 1 Corinthians 12:9

14

among the ministries performed by Christians. And, just as in the other passage, it seems wholly implausible to regard these as a list of official ministries. Prophecy, service, teaching, exhortation, contributing liberally, giving aid, acting in mercy; this is a list in which activities which could (but which need not) be classed as official ministries are placed side by side with activities which could not possibly be so classified.

There is one other passage very like these two which should perhaps be added to them. It occurs in the letter to the Ephesians. This letter may not be by Paul, but if it is not then its author was one who had a good understanding of Pauline thought. It follows an exhortation to meekness and mutual love and also invokes the thought of the church as the body of Christ to explain the significance of the ministry (Eph. 4:4–7, 11–12):

> There is one body and one Spirit, just as you were called to the one hope that belongs to your call, one Lord, one faith, one baptism, one God and Father of us all, who is above all and through all and in all. But grace was given to each of us according to the measure of Christ's gift. . . . And his gifts were that some should be apostles, some prophets, some evangelists, some pastors and teachers, for the equipment of the saints, for the work of ministry, for building up the body of Christ.

Here the list—apostles, prophets, evangelists, pastors and teachers—looks slightly more like a list of official ministries, though it gives no hint of a pattern of ministry such as did later emerge. The author does not say 'some bishops, some presbyters, some deacons' nor 'some ministers, some deacons, some elders'. And the context and doctrinal intention of the passage are exactly that of the other two passages. It looks very much as if the concept of ministry is just the same as that of 1 Corinthians and Romans, though the particular ministries have developed a little.

But what concerns us here is what Paul and deutero-Paul (if it be he) mean by ministries. Paul himself calls them *charismata* (Rom. 12:6; 1 Cor. 12:4,9,28,30,31) and ends 1 Corinthians 12 by saying 'Aspire to the higher *charismata*'. It should surely be perfectly obvious that there is in these three passages no question at all of offices to which people may be appointed. It is

15

only by a forced and unnatural interpretation that such a state of affairs can be read into these passages. Paul's words reflect a situation where there is no official ministry, no distinction between laity and clergy. The order which is evident in the fact that apostles are always mentioned first when they appear and prophets next to them and teachers or some such function third is not a hierarchical but a chronological order. Apostles come first because they are the people who plant the church, be it in Corinth or in Rome or in Ephesus. The church, once founded, is built up by the utterance of prophets and the doctrine of teachers or evangelists. There are several parallels for the use of 'apostle', meaning not necessarily one of the twelve but the man or woman who first plants the Christian faith and so founds the Christian church in any place: Paul himself is of course the supreme example (Rom. 1:1; 11:13; 1 Cor. 1:1; 9:1, 2, 5; 15:9; 2 Cor. 1:1; 11:5; 12:11, 12; Gal. 1:1; Col. 1:1); Andronicus and Junias are others (Rom. 16:7); Apollos another (1 Cor. 4:9); two unnamed men (2 Cor. 8:23); Epaphroditus (Gal. 2:25); Silvanus and Timothy (1 Thess. 1:1 and 2:6) are still others. At Acts 14:4, 14 the author of Acts suddenly calls Paul and Barnabas apostles.

It is important to realize that the ministry envisaged in the three passages examined above is one entirely of function, not of office or ordination. Nobody could ordain anyone to have faith, and if the churches today could ordain people to give liberally or to utter wisdom there would be far more ordinations than there are. It is even incongruous to imagine anyone being ordained as a prophet. Prophets are known by their capacity to utter prophetic sayings, as speakers with tongues and interpreters of tongues are known by their functions, and healers by their capacity to heal.

Ministry in Paul's time is a matter of what we today call charisma. It is something given by the Holy Spirit to the individual for the benefit of the whole local Christian community. It is not an office to which the person endowed with a charisma succeeds. It does not confer permanent authority. Ministry of this sort is occasional and purely functional; it rests upon gifts either natural or supernatural; it is directed by the Spirit who endows different people with different talents to contribute to the common life. These gifts and talents may constitute tasks and duties like administration or leadership or teaching, or they may consist of virtues such as faith and generosity and compassion, or of unusual capacities such as speaking with tongues or discerning spirits. But all these are indiscriminately put on the same level, and they cannot reasonably be regarded as ministerial offices such as those of bishop, priest, deacon or even minister or pastor as we think of them today. In short, in Paul's day the ministry as we know it today did not exist in the church; the distinction between clergy and laity did not exist then.

It is indeed true that we are granted glimpses of the beginning of another sort of ministry even at a quite early period. Paul in Philippians 1:1 refers to 'the bishops and deacons' in that church, though this may mean no more than 'inspectors and helpers'. Luke once represents Paul and Barnabas as appointing presbyters in the churches which they have founded (Acts 14:23), though we cannot be sure that Luke is not reading back into Paul's day conditions which prevailed when he was writing, for Paul in his letters never refers to presbyters. It is likely that there were presbyters in the church of Jerusalem from a very early period; the presbyterate has several analogies within Judaism (as well as within other cultures). Paul is represented by Luke as summoning the presbyters of the church of Ephesus to him at Miletus (Acts 20:17), though in the speech which he makes to them he calls them bishops (20:28). Again, Luke in Acts 6 describes the apostles as appointing seven men to relieve them of their administrative duties so that they could be free for preaching and for prayer. It was from an early period universally assumed that these men were deacons. But Luke does not call them deacons and the only two of whom we know more than their names (Stephen and Philip) do not behave in the least like administrators, but on the contrary are active speakers and evangelists.

In short, though officials such as presbyters were to be found in some places in the church from an early period, we have no reason to assume that they were either universal or essential, and indeed the concept of ministry to be found in Paul's letters is not compatible with such an assumption. An official, permanent ministry, in which ordained men succeed to office, was a development in the life of the church, as the

17

canon of the New Testament was a development, as the creed was a development, as liturgy and monarchical episcopacy were developments.

Authority in the Primitive Church

The result of this investigation of ministry in the earliest period of the church's life is one calculated to disappoint the hopes and claims of almost all the denominations of today. All have been long accustomed to reading their own structures of ministry into the earliest period of Christianity. Where they cannot claim that Christ or his apostles directly instituted a ministry which was in its essentials the form of ministry which they enjoy today (whether papal, episcopal, presbyterian or other), they claim at least that their form of ministry is recognizably present at the very beginning among other forms of ministry which have since died out. Every such claim must be disallowed, in view of the evidence of the Pauline epistles which stands solidly between any modern form of ministry, no matter how ancient, how much hallowed by time, and the earliest age of the church. This means that the two favourite doctrines of both Catholics and Protestants are equally unrealistic, the doctrine of apostolic succession and the doctrine of a scriptural ministry. If official ministry, which is ministry as we know it today in almost any form, did not exist in the earliest phase of the church's growth, then official permanent ministry is a development and must be judged on other grounds and by other criteria than the simple test of whether it was instituted by Christ or his apostles or whether it was there from the very beginning.

But if these conclusions are accepted a very natural question will probably arise in the mind of the reader. Was there no authority in the primitive church? Did it exist somehow in a state of anarchy? Some scholars have been content to answer the last question in the affirmative. Rudolf Sohm, for instance, envisaged the primitive church as living a life completely free from the trammels of authority, of law, of a fixed body of doctrine, in an ideal condition of spontaneous, eschatological, charismatic chaos (See J. L. Adams 'Rudolf Sohm's Theology of Law and Spirit' in *Religion and Culture*, pages 226–7 and 234–5). If one takes a superficial look at the evidence for early Christian worship in 1 Corinthians 10–14 it would be easy to assume that the primitive Christians worshipped in an atmosphere of what might be called sanctified disorder. But in fact a careful reading of the New Testament suggests a different state of affairs. One of the most striking features of the primitive church is the confidence in their own authority displayed by the small, struggling Christian communities of that period. Paul was not inclined to underestimate his authority as an apostle. Indeed, in most of his letters he contends vigorously for it, and especially in 2 Corinthians and in Galatians. But, as Hans von Campenhausen has pointed out in his book, *Ecclesiastical Authority and Spiritual Power in the Church of the First Three Centuries* (Chap. III and IV, especially pages 46 and 70), Paul's conception of apostolic authority carefully leaves the congregations which he has founded free to make their own decisions. If the reader will pardon a quotation from an earlier work of my own, now out of print, *Groundwork for Unity* (pages 23–24), the point can be put more succinctly:

> In spite of his great personal authority as founder and father of his churches, Paul never builds on this relationship 'any spiritual command and hierarchy' (Von Campenhausen), never makes himself into an official, wielding authority. On the contrary,—'not that we lord it over your faith' (2 Cor. 1:24), 'For you were called to freedom, brethren' (Gal. 5:13). Paul insists upon the freedom of his converts in Christ being understood and exercised. He carefully refuses to turn his authority into something official and carefully allows responsibility to his converts. This is because the apostle is constituted by and lives for Christ and only exists so that Christ shall be testified to and reached through him. His personal authority as a man or official is nothing. Consequently, the early church is quite free from regulated hierarchical or ecclesiastical stratification. The Spirit of Christ does not lead to the self-esteem of independence but to service in love.

The Christians of the earliest age were able, in a manner which we find difficult to understand and more difficult to recapture, to reconcile and combine freedom and authority, spontaneity and consent. The book of Acts gives us pictures of the primitive church deciding to replace with a substitute (not a successor) the unfaithful Judas; appointing the seven; sending out Paul and Barnabas; taking counsel about the terms upon which Gentiles were to be admitted to the church; organizing a rudimentary form of communism. Paul (an earlier witness) shows the primitive church debating about meat offered to idols, about marriage regulations, about order in worship; above all he shows that the church was confident enough to exercise that most important form of authority, the forgiving or not forgiving of sins, admitting people to communion or excommunicating them. The whole policy is summed up in Luke's unforgettable words (Acts 2:42), 'And they devoted themselves to the apostles' teaching and fellowship, to the breaking of bread and the prayers'. Olaf Linton, in a book, *Das Problem der Urkirche in neuerer Forschung*, written as long ago as 1932, pointed out the remarkable manner in which the communities of the early church apparently came to their decisions, by a unanimous vote which was neither achieved by head-counting in the modern democratic manner, nor was forced by coercion physical or psychological, the nearest modern analogy to which is probably the way in which committees of the Society of Friends reach their decisions.

Authority in the primitive church, then, did not reside in official ministers but in the church as a whole, all of whose members felt themselves under the authority of Christ. The apostle of the church, as both the spiritual father (1 Cor. 4:14,15) and mother (Gal. 4:19) of his converts, can guide them, exhort them, attempt to persuade or shame them into a course of action; he can rebuke them as well as praise them. But he allows that authority resides in the church as a whole. If anybody appears bearing authority, this is authority delegated to him by the church, and this possibility of delegation no doubt accounts for the beginning of the official ministry. The manner in which the early Christians decided matters is vividly presented in a vignette in Matthew 18:15–17, which gives us, not the words of Jesus, but the experience of the primitive church:

> If your brother sins against you, go and tell him his fault, between you and him alone. If he listens to you, you have gained your brother. But if he does not listen, take one or two others along

20

with you, that every word may be confirmed by the evidence of two or three witnesses. If he refuses to listen to them, tell it to the church; and if he refuses to listen even to the church, let him be to you as a Gentile and a tax collector.

But even when official ministry was well established, the tradition remained that it was the whole church which possessed authority. Letters from Christian officials in the 2nd century are almost all addressed not in the name of individual bishops or presbyters but in the name of the whole church. The forgiving of sins long remained something which concerned the whole church; Hermas and the author of II Clement, both of whom are concerned about discipline in the church, both witness to this conviction. Still in Tertullian's day the penitent seeking admission to communion after a lapse must show his penitence in an unmistakable way not just to the bishop but to the local Christian congregation assembled. Indeed it is long before the tradition completely dies out that forgiveness of sins is the prerogative of the whole church, not just of the minister.

Finally, even in the time of Cyprian, who probably did more than anybody else in the church of the first three centuries to establish the independent authority of the official minister, it is a firmly entrenched tradition that the people (the *plebs*) must be consulted on certain important decisions, such as the choice of a bishop. And Cyprian expects the congregations of bishops who have sinned a grievous sin, such as apostasy during persecution, to take the initiative in withdrawing from their communion. These are the lingering remnants of the primitive consciousness that Christ's authority resided not in the minister in his own right by virtue of his office being instituted by Christ, but in the whole church, at a time when no uniform or universal official ministry had yet emerged.

The Priesthood of Christ

We can now resume the theme of Christian priesthood. It was necessary first to spend some time establishing the proper principles and assumptions with which the subject should be

21

approached if it is to be treated with neither ecclesiastical bias nor inherited prejudice nor partiality, but with honest judgment and scholarly truth. The first point to observe is that according to the New Testament Christ is a high priest, indeed the high priest, of a new and permanent order. There had, of course, been speculations and expectations about the advent of a priestly Messiah before the birth of Christ. The people of the Dead Sea Scrolls, the Qumran Covenanters as they are sometimes called, had expected two Messiahs. One was to be of Aaron's line, i.e. belonging to the Levitical priests of the time who were all supposed to be of the same clan and who were responsible for the conduct of the worship, sacrifice and ordering of the temple in Jerusalem, even though the Covenanters had fallen out with that worship and claimed themselves to represent a better, purer, less corrupt form of worship and of priesthood than the Sadducean priests who had possession of the temple in their time. The other Messiah was to be a descendant of David, a warrior Messiah.

No writer in the New Testament claims that Jesus was of the tribe of Levi or a descendant of Aaron. Manifestly the facts themselves would contradict such a claim. The genealogies of Christ in both Matthew and Luke's gospels make out that Jesus was a descendant of David and of the patriarch Judah, and both curiously draw his genealogy through Joseph, not through Mary. But whatever these genealogies mean (and on the face of it they are inconsistent with the story of the Virgin Birth of Jesus), they are not intended to claim for Jesus that he was of the Levitical priesthood. There is one puzzling passage in Mark (12:35–37) where Jesus asks a question with the apparent purpose of showing that the Christ could not come from David's line. If Jesus was claiming to be the Christ, this passage would imply that he was not, and knew he was not, a descendant of David. If this is a saying put into the mouth of Jesus by somebody during the period of oral transmission of the gospel material, then this person knew, or thought he knew, that Jesus was not descended from David.

The genealogies of Matthew and Luke are highly untrustworthy as historical information. We are left therefore with no satisfactory evidence that Jesus himself could claim in any sense to be descended from ancestors who were priests of the temple in Jerusalem, and only with ambiguous evidence that he even claimed to be descended from David.

But we can be in no doubt that Jesus was thought to be a high priest. The classic exposition of this theme is of course in the epistle to the Hebrews (4:14–10:18). Indeed this theme may be said to constitute the chief subject of this work. The author to the Hebrews (who, it need hardly be said, is not Paul) sees Christ as the inaugurator of a new type of priesthood, associated, not with Levi nor with Aaron, but with Melchizedek, that strange figure mentioned in Genesis 14:17–20, as 'priest of God Most High' (*El Elyon*) who met Abraham after his defeat of Chedorlaomer and three other local kings, offered him bread and wine, blessed him, and received from him 'a tenth of everything'.

Interest in this figure of Melchizedek was not confined to the author to the Hebrews. The figure of Melchizedek also appears in one of the documents of the Dead Sea Scrolls, and speculation concerning him can be found in fragments of Christian literature surviving from Christian writers of the late 2nd and early 3rd centuries who wish to develop a specifically Christian doctrine of God without invoking the aid of a Logos doctrine. They may well have inherited such a tradition independently of the epistle to the Hebrews. Interest in Melchizedek evidently sprang from a Judaeo-Christian tradition or speculation which could be used in different ways in different circles. The author to the Hebrews either associated or identified Christ with Melchizedek. In a typically rabbinic fashion he assumes Melchizedek to have had no father or mother because the meagre narrative in Genesis does not happen to mention his parents (Heb. 7:3). This ancient priest was either thought to be the form in which the pre-incarnate Christ appeared to Abraham (not at all an impossible concept for a writer in the New Testament), or some super-human being who prefigured Christ as the new high priest.

The chief point which the author to the Hebrews wishes to make by his introduction of this theme of a priesthood after the order of Melchizedek is to contrast Christ's priesthood with that of the Levitical, Aaronic or Sadducean priesthood. It is almost impossible to determine whether the temple at Jerusalem was still standing when the author to the Hebrews

23

wrote his work and the whole elaborate apparatus of cult and sacrifice still operating. But if he wrote after 70AD, he cannot have been writing long after the destruction of the temple by the Romans, and expects most of the details of the cult to be fresh in the minds of his readers, or at least (for he is not himself completely accurate in his references to the cult) that they shall be well acquainted with the Pentateuch and the cultic legislation in it.

For him Christ has superseded the Jewish sacrificial cult. Whether it still operates or not, it has lost its significance. It was temporary, material, at the best a prefiguring, unable to achieve permanent reconciliation with God for its practisers. Christ's priesthood is permanent, indeed eternal, spiritual not material, and effective, so that it has achieved salvation for those who are involved in the new Christian cult. Christ's priestly activity is also final. There is no further need of continuing, daily renewed sacrifice or offering. His intercession makes all other forms of intercession unnecessary. His priesthood as expounded in the epistle to the Hebrews might be described as a priesthood to end priesthoods.

The epistle to the Hebrews is much more absorbed with the idea of Christ as priest than is any other writer in the New Testament; but the idea is not absent. Mark's record (15:37,38) that at the death of Jesus the veil of the temple was torn from top to bottom is surely meant to imply that with the death of this victim all cultic sacrifices of victims according to the Jewish law now ceased to have any significance. John's careful placing of the time of the crucifixion on the day before the Passover feast so that it coincides with the period at which the lambs would be slaughtered in the temple in preparation for the Passover, the frequent references in Revelation to Jesus as the slaughtered lamb associated with a heavenly throne or altar, all these must be taken as pointing in the same direction. It seems likely that the garment which the figure of Jesus is wearing in Revelation 1:13 is a high–priestly garment. Paul does not develop a specific theology of Christ as high priest, but the whole thrust of his thought is towards the conclusion that 'Christ is the end of the law' (Rom. 10:4, *telos* = both fulfilment and stop). After he has offered himself in supreme obedience, no other offering could be of significance. The
24

whole complex sacrificial system is superseded by what he has achieved.

In a more general sense, the genius of early Christianity tends towards a playing down of the legal and cultic and an enhancing of the prophetic elements in the Judaism which it had inherited and in the sacred scriptures which it took over as the legacy of Judaism. When the Jewish sacrificial cult was finally ended by the fall of Jerusalem to the Romans in 70 AD Judaism suffered a shock which was severe even though it was not fatal. The Pharisaic party was able to reconstruct Judaism on quite a new basis, but the idea of a Jewish national state centred on Jerusalem and on the temple in Jerusalem died hard; it involved the Jews in several unsuccessful and damaging uprisings in later years. But Christianity appears to have suffered no lasting shock from this event. Cultic sacrifice such as the Jews practised, and such as several pagan religions in different forms also practised, formed by then no essential part of Christianity at all. Cultic priests and sacrifices on altars appeared at that point to be irrelevant to the serious concerns of Christianity.

The Priesthood of All Believers

There is a doctrine of priesthood, however, which is entirely consistent with the concept of Christ's new and permanent priesthood and which can easily be reconciled with the abolition of the Jewish cult, and this doctrine is to be found clearly evidenced in the New Testament. This is what is conventionally called 'the priesthood of all believers'. There are four passages in the New Testament which are always cited to support this doctrine, though in fact it has much firmer support than merely these four. They run as follows:

> Come to him, to that living stone, rejected by men but in God's sight chosen and precious; and like living stones be yourselves built into a spiritual house, to be a holy priesthood, to offer spiritual sacrifices acceptable to God through Jesus Christ. . . . But you are a chosen race, a royal priesthood, a holy nation, God's own people, that you may declare the wonderful deeds of him who called you out of darkness into his marvellous light. (1 Peter 2:4–5, 9)

To him who loves us and has freed us from our sins by his blood and made us a kingdom, priests to his God and Father, to him be glory and dominion for ever and ever. Amen. (Revelation 1:5, 6)

And they sang a new song, saying,
'Worthy art thou to take the scroll and to open its seals,
for thou wast slain and by thy blood didst ransom men for God
from every tribe and tongue and people and nation,
and hast made them a kingdom and priests to our God,
and they shall reign on earth.' (Rev. 5:9, 10)

Blessed and holy is he who shares in the first resurrection! Over such the second death has no power, but they shall be priests of God and of Christ, and they shall reign with him a thousand years. (Rev. 20:6)

This is a doctrine of what might be called a collective priesthood. All Christians together constitute a priestly body whose business is to be the medium or expression of Christ's priesthood, to declare the message of this reconciliation between God and man achieved through him. In fact such a doctrine as this is to be found in different forms in several other parts of the New Testament. It appears when Paul uses priestly or cultic language of his own activity in spreading the gospel:

But on some points I have written to you very boldly by way of reminder, because of the grace given me by God to be a minister of Christ Jesus to the Gentiles in the priestly service of the gospel of God, so that the offering of the Gentiles may be acceptable, sanctified by the Holy Spirit. (Rom. 15:15, 16)

The concept of Christians as priests offering spiritual sacrifices is also to be found in the well-known words of Romans 12:1:

I appeal to you therefore, brethren, by the mercies of God, to present your bodies as a living sacrifice, holy and acceptable to God, which is your spiritual worship.

In fact it is not difficult to see in many more passages of Paul that Christians regard themselves as a chosen people, picked out in order to proclaim the great message of God's salvation at the end of the world, and that this calling and obligation makes them conscious of being a peculiar people, set aside and consecrated as priests are consecrated for this holy task. The concept of Christians as a holy temple, which appears side by

26

side with the doctrine of Christians' priesthood in the passage from 1 Peter quoted above, echoes this:

> For we are the temple of the living God; as God said,
>   'I will live in them and move among them,
>   and I will be their God
>   and they shall be my people.
>   Therefore come out from them
>   and be separate from them, says the Lord,
>   and touch nothing unclean;
>   then I will welcome you,
>   and I will be a father to you,
>   and you shall be my sons and daughters
>   says the Lord Almighty.' (2 Cor. 6:16-18)

It is easily seen that this idea of the priesthood of Christians is one aspect of that self-confidence and sense of authority which characterizes the behaviour of the primitive church in other parts of its life. It is part of that sense of common mission and destiny which gave the early church its authority and its capacity to exercise that authority. It is, as we have seen, a mistake to imagine that in the primitive church there was no authority. The fact is that this authority was regarded as collective or communal or organic rather than as residing in permanent officials. And if we are to be consistent we must conclude (and in later pages of this book we shall develop this theme) that even when permanent official ministries emerge, they are still no more than (one could equally well say no less than) offices representative of and bearing authority delegated to them by the whole Christian people. They are not offices instituted independently of the rest of the church by Christ or his apostles, offices whose holders bear rule over the church by an independent line of authority deriving from Christ.

To put the matter in another way, when Christ founded the church he made no distinction between clergy and laity in it. This is not to say that this distinction is necessarily wrong, but only that it is not of dominical nor apostolic institution. As permanent official ministers arose out of the life and needs of the church, so such ministers never had any justification for claiming (often though this claim was made) that their authority was anything else than authority delegated by the whole church. When the author of 1 Clement writes to the whole

27

church of Corinth to protest against their irresponsible deposition of presbyters, at some point quite early in the 2nd century, he does not argue that only presbyters can depose presbyters, that the laity have no power over the clergy (even though he certainly recognizes the distinction between clergy and laity), but that the laity must not depose clergy irresponsibly, for insufficient reasons.

It has been usual for writers of the Free Church or non-episcopal persuasion to argue stoutly for the doctrine of the priesthood of all believers and for writers of the Roman Catholic and Anglican traditions to underestimate it. I was myself guilty of playing down this doctrine in my earlier book, *Groundwork for Unity*. But I now realize that a closer look at the early fathers will reveal traces of this doctrine in many places and make it plain that this was a conviction which remained vigorous and living for several centuries after New Testament times. It is not, it must be added, the doctrine—which has sometimes been represented as the true version of this doctrine—that every Christian is a priest in the sense of an official minister. This would be to commit the curious anomaly of reading the existence of official ministers into the earliest age of the church in order to discredit the authority of one kind of official ministers, priests. Even though Tertullian may do precisely this, he is alone in this application of the doctrine and is inconsistent in applying it thus. The priesthood of all believers means that as the church has the authority of Christ in ministering and so can delegate that authority to ministers whose authority rests on that of the church, so the church can delegate its priestly authority to official priests whose authority rests upon the priesthood of Christ expressed in and through the priestly authority of the church. But this is to anticipate.

We have already noticed that among the Christian literature of the 2nd century the writers of letters almost always write in the name of the church which they represent. We have seen that the author of the 1 Clement did so. Ignatius writes to the bishops of the churches of Ephesus, Tralles, Magnesia, Philadelphia and Philippi but he does so as a means of greeting the whole church, and his greeting is the greeting of the church of Antioch as a whole; and Dionysius of Corinth follows the same convention in those letters of his of which Eusebius the ecclesiastical historian has preserved fragments (*Historia Ecclesiastica* II.25.8; IV.23.1–12). A clear doctrine of the priesthood of all Christians emerges in Justin who says that all Christians are 'a high priestly race' who offer acceptable sacrifices to God (Dialogue 116.3). We can find the same doctrine in Irenaeus. He says that the apostles were justified in plucking ears of corn on the sabbath day (Luke 6:3,4) because they were all priests and priests were allowed to do this (1 Sam. 21:4ff), and he adds that all their disciples ever since were priests, and by these he means all Christians ever since (*Adversus Haereses* IV:17). He refers to this passage in a later part of the work and maintains that references to Levites and priests really mean the disciples of the Lord (V.34.3).

Tertullian in this respect constitutes a special case, because he was a passionate advocate of the Montanists and was in consequence strongly prejudiced against the official clergy of the Catholic Church and especially in his latest writings against one particular bishop, whether Callistus of Rome or Agrippinus of Carthage it is difficult to say. Still, even in those books written in the middle period of his writing career, when he is not writing in a specifically Montanist interest, the doctrine of the priesthood of all believers can be found. He says in *Adversus Marcionem* (III.7.7) that one of the goats mentioned in Leviticus 16 represents the second coming of Christ, at which, 'when all sins have been expiated the priests of the spiritual temple, that is the church, enjoy as it were a kind of public banquet of the Lord's grace, while the rest are fasting from salvation'. Later in the same book (IV.23.10,11) he says that the words of Jesus recorded in Luke 9:60, 'Let the dead bury their dead,' meant that the Lord 'was training for worship and priesthood the man whom he had apprenticed by preaching the kingdom of God'.

In his later works, as the rigorism of Montanism grips him more strongly, he returns to this doctrine more frequently. He recognizes in all his works a distinction between clergy (*ordo*, embracing, as we shall see, *sacerdotes*), including the *De Exhortatione Castitatis*, which is written to dissuade Christians from remarrying after their first spouses have died. But he finds it useful in this work to stress the priesthood of the laity, and he

29

interprets this to mean that, not only can a layman exorcize (X.2; XI.7), but at times he writes as if priest's orders are nothing but sheer convenience (VIII.1–4), and in another work (*De Fuga in Persecutione* XIV.1) he declares that in an emergency any three Christians, lay or clerical, can celebrate the eucharist. Another late work of his written against the re-marriage of Christians, *De Monogamia*, has several passages spiritedly maintaining the doctrine of the priesthood of all believers (VIII.7; XII.1–5; cf; *Adversus Judaeos* XIV.9).

That Tertullian in maintaining this doctrine was not merely indulging a Montanist quirk, even though his Montanism led him to over-emphasize it, is shown by its appearance in writers later than Tertullian who are not likely to have been influenced by his works. In Hippolytus' *Apostolic Tradition* one sentence in the bishop's prayer at an ordination runs, 'we offer to thee the bread and the cup making eucharist to thee because thou hast made us worthy to stand before thee and minister as priests to thee' (16 in the reconstruction of Dom Bernard Botte, which I follow here). The plural 'priests' suggests that the bishop here can hardly be thought to be speaking for himself alone, as even the episcopal 'we' would not describe the bishop as plural here; he is probably referring to all the congregation, on whose behalf he is offering the bread and the wine as priests. Clement of Alexandria echoes the doctrine when he declares that all gnostic (i.e. fully initiated or educated) Christians are priests (*hiereis*, *Stromateis* VII.7.36; compare V.6.39), and that only those who live purely are priests (IV.25.158).

Later Origen teaches the doctrine of the priesthood of all believers, as the latest book on Origen's doctrine of the Church, *Das Kirchenverständnis des Origenes* (Böhlau Verlag, Cologne and Vienna 1974), a fine study by Josef Vogt, makes clear (see pages 111–117 and references cited there). As in the case of other traditional doctrines which he inherited, Origen gave this doctrine his own individual interpretation, in accordance with the tendency in all his thought to spiritualize doctrine and refer it to inward experience, but that he took it to be part of the body of conventional Christian teaching is clear.

Others Priests in the New Testament

Having investigated the origins of the concept of ministry in the early church, and the nature of the authority of the church at that period, and having traced the doctrine of the priesthood of Christ in the New Testament and that of the priesthood of of all believers from the period of the New Testament to the middle of the 3rd century, we must now ask the question, 'Does the New Testament recognize any individual minister as a Christian priest in virtue of his being a minister?' The reader will not be surprised to find that this question must receive as answer an emphatic negative. Priests are of course mentioned in the New Testament. The priests who were occupied in the service of the cult at the temple in Jerusalem are referred to again and again, and even some of them are said to have become Christians (Acts 6:7). The Jewish high priest takes a prominent part in the trial of Jesus in the four gospels, and appears at times later in Acts, even as late as the encounter of the high priest Ananias with Paul (23:1–5).

In particular, there is a group referred to as 'the high priests' many times in the gospels and Acts. These were ex-high priests, for during the 1st century the Roman rulers of Palestine thought it expedient frequently to depose the current high priest and replace him by a man, chosen duly from the high-priestly family, thought for the moment to be more suitable. There could never be more than one high priest functioning at any moment, but there always were as a consequence of this policy several former high priests surviving. With these are sometimes associated members of the high-priestly family, whether they had been high priests or not (e.g. Acts 4:6). These all apparently formed a distinct group who were regarded as concerting counsel and following the same policy. There is also mention once of a less reputable high priest, 'a Jewish high priest named Sceva' (Acts 19:14); this is a man who calls himself 'high priest' in a very general and unofficial way, much as many American lawyers used apparently to call themselves 'judge' without exercising any official judicial functions. And finally there is one mention in the New Testament of a pagan high priest, the priest of Zeus at Lystra, who, when Paul had healed a cripple there 'brought oxen and

31

garlands to the gates and wanted to offer sacrifice with the people', but was prevented by the indignant remonstrance of Paul and Barnabas (Acts 14:13).

There is no mention of Christian officials as priests whatever. We have no ground for assuming that the large number of priests of the Jewish temple who, we are told, became Christians officiated as or were regarded as priests in any specifically Christian sense. Despairing attempts have been made to read the existence of Christian priests into various parts of the New Testament. For instance at Acts 13:1, 2 Luke tells us that five persons, Barnabas, Symeon, Lucius, Manaen and Saul (i.e. Paul) who were at Antioch, were worshipping and fasting, and the Greek word for 'worshipping' (*leitour-gountōn*) could be used for a priestly cultic worship. But in fact Paul uses a cognate word (*leitourgon*), as we have already seen, to describe his ministry of the gospel (Rom. 15:16), where he certainly does not think of himself as an official priest. There is no reason to read into the verb used in Acts 13:2 a sacerdotal or hierarchical meaning which would create an isolated and unparallelled example. Luke calls these men prophets and teachers, not priests, and it would be unprecedented, not only to envisage an official priesthood emerging as early as this, but to assume that any permanent officials of any sort had yet appeared to maintain the ministry of the gospel.

There is no other part of the New Testament where a mention of Christian official priests is even remotely likely. We can indeed see in the later books of the New Testament evidence for the gradual development of an official ministry of bishops, presbyters, and deacons, though the process was by no means complete when the latest book of the New Testament was written. But of official Christian priests we must honestly admit there is in the New Testament not the faintest whisper.

2

THE EMERGENCE OF A CHRISTIAN PRIESTHOOD

An Official Ministry Emerges

The precise manner in which an official ministry developed in the early church has been treated extensively in other works, and is not the theme of this book. It is enough to understand that the appearance of a ministry in which permanent office-bearers succeeded each other in office and were appointed by some formal act of ordination was a development in the life of the church. These office-bearers were not there at the beginning, and when they do exercise authority it is authority exercised as representing the church and as delegated to them by the church. They do not derive their authority in a direct historical line of succession from Christ or his apostles independently of the rest of the church.

One point about this official ministry, however, needs to be made clear before we can proceed further in our argument. It is a universal tendency in the Christian religion, as in many other religions, to give a theological interpretation to institutions which have developed gradually through a period of time for the sake of practical usefulness, and then to read that interpretation back into the earliest periods and infancy of these institutions, attaching them to an age when in fact nobody imagined that they had such a meaning. The simplest and least controversial example of this is the case of ecclesiastical garments, whether these are chasuble, amice, stole and alb or surplice, cope and mitre. Almost all these garments were first assumed for some non-theological reason. Either they were the ordinary wear for grand occasions of a layman of the time when they were adopted, or they were assumed in order to keep the wearer warm in cold climates or cool in hot climates,

33

or they even (as in the case of the mitre) had originally a political rather than a theological significance. But in later ages religious fancy set to work on them and attributed to them all sorts of edifying theological reasons and symbolism: they stood for humility, for purity, they were emblems of the yoke of Christ or the linen towel with which he girded himself at the last supper, and so on.

The same fate has befallen the various forms of official ministry which emerged and became permanent or well established in the 2nd century. They attracted to themselves in later ages all sorts of theological significance of which the the 2nd century was unaware, some part of which this book will study. And the fact that the major ministries, bishop, priest and deacon, were three in number was regarded—and still is regarded by those who stoutly defend the threefold ministry—as peculiarly significant, whereas to the eye of the historian it appears largely adventitious.

As a kind of modern counterpart to this perennial tendency, scholars for the last hundred years have laboured to find antecedents to the office of bishop, of presbyter and of deacon in every possible place. Except that the council of presbyters was an already existing, not very prominent or significant Jewish institution, these attempts all seem to me to have failed; and the reason for their failure is obvious. There is no need to examine the Old Testament, to search through the records of the Qumran Covenanters, to ransack the pages of Josephus, to search Hellenistic culture or look to the institution of Jewish high priest in order to find analogies and predecessors for bishops, presbyters and deacons. The early church adopted that form of ministry which it found most convenient and which best suited its immediate needs and condition, and in giving these ministries names it had no particular regard to theological consistency or significance, nor was it greatly concerned to preserve and perpetuate existing institutions or offices.

The proof of this is twofold: first, the very large number of antecedents which speculative scholars claim to have found for them; their very number reduces their plausibility to nothing; second, the general and widely applicable nature of the three offices themselves. For us the words bishops, presbyters and deacons are stored with the associations of nearly two thousand years. For the people who first used them the titles of these offices can have meant little more than inspectors, older men and helpers. It was to the church's advantage that these three ministries entered the centuries to come unencumbered, so to speak, with theological baggage. As we shall see, it was when unsuitable theological significance began to be attached to them that the distortion of the concept of Christian ministry began.

The Second Century

No Christian priesthood is to be found in the New Testament. There is in fact no solid evidence that anyone thinks of Christian ministers as priests until about the year 200. Attempts have been made to find evidence for a Christian priesthood in the 2nd century. If some passages can plausibly be dressed up to appear like evidence for a Christian priesthood in the 2nd century, then it might be possible to interpret passages in the New Testament which are not apparently favourable to this interpretation as in reality favouring it, and so the blessed haven of an apostolic or dominical institution for the priesthood might be reached.

One of the most often cited passages in this connection is that from the *Didache* (13,3) which runs, 'You must grant the first-fruit to the prophets, for they are your high priests' (*archiereis*). The reference is a puzzling one and its meaning has not been convincingly divined by any scholar so far. One difficulty confronting all users of the *Didache* is the date of the book. Conjectures have ranged from as early as about 60 AD (for at least part of the book) to as late as the second half of the 2nd century. At the moment scholarly opinion may be said to be verging towards placing the *Didache* in the 2nd century rather than the 1st, but it is impossible to come to a confident conclusion here. The book certainly shows much Jewish influence; it might even be thought of as a piece of early Judaeo-Christian literature, to employ the useful classification suggested by the late Cardinal J. Daniélou (in *The Theology of Jewish Christianity*). This would make the reference to high priests more understandable. But all Jews would know that there could never have been more than one functioning high priest at the same time; this is the rock upon which Arnold Ehrhardt's attempt (in *The Apostolic Succession*) to derive bishops from the Jewish high priest struck. Perhaps the plural suggests a community which treasures Jewish traditions and institutions but which has become through lapse of time a little remote from them. The enigma of this sentence remains. But it certainly cannot be held to point to the existence of Christian official ministers who were regarded as priests.

As has been already observed, it is difficult to imagine prophets being ordained. Likely candidates for the position of priest in the 2nd century should be presbyters or bishops. But nobody called these priests at that time. Another passage which has been cited in order to make a case for the existence of Christian priests in the 2nd century is Ignatius' *Letter to the Philippians* chapter 9, section 1, 'The priests (*hiereis*) are also good, but the high priest is better'. Could Ignatius here mean the presbyters by the priests and the bishop by the high priest? But the context shows clearly enough what Ignatius means. The priests are the priests of the Old Testament. The high priest is Christ. Ignatius is declaring the superiority of Christ as the final high priest to the priestly ministry of the cult officials of the old dispensation, much in the same line of argument as that deployed in the epistle to the Hebrews. There can be no basis for a Christian priesthood in the 2nd century here.

The author of the I Clement at first sight appears a likely candidate for the earliest writer to mention a Christian priesthood, and several reputable scholars have actually come to the conclusion that he did so. We must, it should be noted, free ourselves from the idea which has long prevailed that this work can be dated by the writer's connection with Flavius Clemens the consul who was executed by the Emperor Domitian in 96 AD. Paul Keresztes seems to me to have satisfactorily shown that Flavius Clemens' association is much more likely to have been with Judaism than with Christianity. We can therefore place it later than 96 AD, up to any point about the middle of the 2nd century, perhaps about 120.

A long passage in I Clement (chapters 40–44) deals with the

order and distinctions within the ministry which God desired to establish under the old dispensation. The writer particularly emphasizes the different ranks of high priest, priest and Levite, and the different duties and function attached to each. His purpose certainly is to impress on the Corinthian Christians (to whom he is writing) the necessity of their maintaining order in their own church and in particular of respecting and preserving the office of presbyter. It has been thought by many that Clement intended in this passage to compare the orders of Christian ministry with the orders of Old Testament ministry, so that bishops might correspond to high priest, presbyter to priest and deacon to Levite.

This, were it true, would indeed be the introduction of something like a Christian priesthood. But in fact such an interpretation of the passage would be not only implausible but on several grounds it is virtually impossible. In the first place, the writer never actually draws such a comparison between the old and the new ministries, and in fact nobody (not even Cyprian) regularly makes so exact a matching of ministries until about two hundred years after Clement's day. Secondly, it would have been impossible for the author of I Clement to make the ministries of the old and new covenants correspond to each other in this way because, while he recognizes three orders of Old Testament ministry, he only knows of two ministries in the Christian church, that of *episkopos*/presbyter (bishop and presbyter being regarded as identical as in Acts 20:28, Hermas, the *Didache* and the Pastoral Epistles in the New Testament), and of deacon. Two cannot correspond to three.

Thirdly—and this seems to me to be the decisive point—in another part of his work Clement gives us his Old Testament proof-text for the Christian ministry, and it has nothing to do with the high priest, priest and Levite of the Jewish cult. It is taken from Isaiah 60:17, and is a curious variant translation of that text, corresponding neither to the Hebrew nor to the LXX version of it. The proof-text runs, 'I will set up their bishops in righteousness and their deacons in faith' (I Clement 42,5). The same text, in the same variant form, is quoted by Irenaeus later (*Adv. Haer.* IV.42.2). Apparently it was a traditional Christian proof-text doctored, as these proof-texts

37

sometimes were, to fit the facts of the case.

It is characteristic of early Christianity that it should take its Old Testament justification for its institutions not from the Law but from the Prophets. But this text confirms the conclusion that I Clement contains no concept of the orders of Christian ministry corresponding to those of the Old Testament cult. All that the author was doing in chapters 40–44 was using an Old Testament example to enforce upon his hearers the general importance of *taxis* (order) in the church. There are no other passages in the Christian literature of the 2nd century that can be said to point with any plausibility to the existence of a Christian priesthood.

The Beginnings of Christian Priesthood

The first writer to speak of Christian ministry in terms of priesthood is Tertullian, about 200 AD. Throughout his works he refers to the bishop as *sacerdos* (priest) or *sacerdos summus* (high priest). He does so without explanation, as if the title was a familiar one to his readers. He occasionally applies the word *sacerdos* to the presbyter also, as when he runs through all the functions of an ordained person, in order to list what it is forbidden for a woman to do; the man may preach (*loqui*), teach (*docere*), baptize (*tinguere*), celebrate the eucharist (*offerre*), but women may not do this, nor take on themselves any masculine function, far less the priestly office (*nec ullius virilis muneris, nedum sacerdotatis officii, sortem sibi vindicare, De Virginibus Velandis* 11,1). Again he writes of a husband who has married a second wife after the death of his first praying for both at the eucharist and says, 'Will you offer for both of them and will you commend both of them through the priest?' (*sacerdotem, De Exhortatione Castitatis* 11,20); here too he may mean a presbyter. But in much the greater number of cases Tertullian designates the bishop when he uses priestly terms. For him evidently the bishop is the priest or the high priest *par excellence*. He also uses the term 'altar' very frequently. Indeed, he can summarize Christian observance as *altare et sacerdos* (altar and priest, *De Ieiuniis ad Psychicos* 16,8). But it is to be observed that Tertullian does not draw any theological infer-
38

ences from this use of the term priest for bishops and presbyters. The term seems to come naturally to his lips, but he does not seem to want to use it in order to build any particular doctrine of the episcopal or presbyteral ministry.

Hippolytus, Tertullian's younger contemporary who wrote in Greek in Rome during the first two decades of the 3rd century, witnesses to the same practice. At the beginning of his long work against heresies, the *Elenchos*, he states uncompromisingly his own claim to be a bishop, declaring that he is a successor of the apostles and (using the episcopal we) 'reckoned to be partakers of the same grace and high priesthood and teaching and guardians of the Church' (I *Praef.* 6). The same sacerdotal language is used about the bishop, but more emphatically, in Hippolytus' *Apostolic Tradition*. This work gives, among other items, a model prayer for the consecration of a bishop; part of it prays to God that the bishop may 'feed thy holy flock and serve as thine high priest . . . that he may unceasingly . . . propitiate thy countenance and offer to thee the gifts of thy holy Church' (3). It seems likely that this high-priestly character of the bishop may have particular reference to his power of forgiving sins, because this power is mentioned again later in the prayer for the consecration of the elements, 'in the high-priestly spirit (*tō pneumati tō archieratikō*) have authority to forgive sins according to thy command' (3).

Hippolytus distinguishes sharply between the functions and powers of a bishop and those of a presbyter, and he seems to be confused about whether a presbyter is a priest or not. The model prayer for ordaining a presbyter contains no mention of his being a priest and the list of his duties specifies only those of sharing the presbyterate and governing the people. The Old Testament type for the presbyter is the elders appointed by Moses (20). Presbyters are to lay hands on at the ordination of a presbyter because of the spirit common to all clergy, but the presbyter in doing this is not ordaining but blessing (*sphragizein*); only the bishop can ordain (*cheirotonein*, 24). The bishop alone is to ordain the deacon, because the deacon 'is not ordained for a priesthood' (which suggests that the presbyter is so ordained), and he is not appointed to be fellow-counsellor with the bishop nor to receive the spirit common to all presbyters (22,24).

39

It is clear that for Hippolytus, even more than for Tertullian, the bishop is the priest *par excellence*. Later in the same work Hippolytus says that the widow is not to be regarded as ordained, because she does not offer the oblation, nor has she a cultic ministry (*leitourgia*). Cultic ministry is for clergy (*klēros*), and the same conditions apply to virgins (30,32). Paul had described himself as a cultic minister and as offering an oblation metaphorically, referring to his evangelizing activity. Hippolytus has transposed this metaphor into literal language.

The same sacerdotal language is applied to the bishop, only perhaps rather more strongly, in the *Didascalia Apostolorum*. This is a work discussing and prescribing, among other matters, the duties of the clergy. It was originally written in Greek but survives today in a Syriac and a fragmentary Latin translation (I quote from Connolly's English translation, first section and then page). Its date cannot be accurately determined beyond saying that it was written in the 3rd century and perhaps in the first rather than the second half of that century. It consistently applies the language of priesthood to the bishop, and particularly emphasizes his power of forgiving sins and allotting penance. It invokes the example of the Old Testament cultic ministry in several places, and once cautiously adduces the example of the pagan high priest (IX, 90–92). It applies to the bishop the text in Numbers 18:1 'Thou and Aaron shall take upon you the sins of the priesthood' (VII, 56). It enjoins that the bishop must be unblemished in body, like the Old Testament high priest, in accordance with Leviticus 21:17 (IV, 32). The example of the Levites is appealed to in commending the practice of the bishop's flock supporting him by their offerings, and immediately afterwards a series of titles is given to the bishop which includes those of Levite and priest (VIII, 80). It is interesting to note that this writer, who knows the text of the *Didache*, reproduces its curious expression 'for they are your high priests', but applies it to bishops, leaving the title priests and Levites to presbyters and deacons, orphans and widows; but at the end of this passage the writer repeats, confusingly, that the bishop is a Levite and high priest (IX, 86). One gains the impression that, though the author of the *Didascalia Apostolorum*, like Tertullian and Hippolytus, regarded the bishop as the priestly officer above all

40

others, he had no consistent doctrine of this priestly ministry. It is, however, clear that by the beginning of the 3rd century it was an established and widely recognized practice in the church to describe Christian clergy, and especially bishops, as priests.

Reasons for the Emergence of a Priesthood

It is appropriate at this point to pause and ask why the doctrine of a Christian priesthood, which is absent from the beginnings of the Christian ministry, should have emerged in the 3rd century. The chief reason, clearly enough, is that it was thought necessary and appropriate in order to express the priestly activity of Christ. Once an official, permanent, ordained ministry had appeared, this next development was, no doubt, inevitable. The priesthood of all believers and the involvement of the whole church in acts of authority are still formally maintained. But once the authority of the church has been channelled and concentrated into an official ministry it is only logical that all the aspects of the church's activity should be expressed in that ministry, and above all in that official who had by 200 become the chief Christian minister, the monarchical bishop. Perhaps it is significant that the epistle to the Hebrews, after Tertullian, who refers to it only once or twice and tends to think that it was written by Barnabas, is totally unused in the western church until the middle of the 4th century. It does not seem to have been very influential in the eastern church during the 3rd century; Clement of Alexandria and Origen in their references to make it clear that its Pauline authorship was not securely established; this must have tended to reduce its influence.

In fact the passage to which authors in the end of the 2nd and in the 3rd century refer in order to establish the priesthood of Christ is usually Zechariah 3:1–5, in which the high priest Joshua changes his filthy garments for clean ones. This was taken to be a reference to Christ's incarnation as high priest of the new dispensation. The bishop would thus naturally tend to be regarded as the representative of Christ and so as a high priest. In him is expressed the priestly function of the church

41

which is a reflection and realization of the priestly activity of Christ. The fact that the control of discipline and penance had by this period gradually fallen into the hands of the bishop would support this way of regarding him, for the activity of the Jewish high priest as described in the Old Testament law was in the minds of Christians peculiarly associated with the forgiveness of sins, not least because of his part in entering alone into the Holy of Holies on the Day of Atonement.

The existence of these law books of the Old Testament may well have constituted another cause of the emergence of a Christian priesthood. As has been remarked more than once already, Christian interpretation of the Hebrew scriptures differed from Jewish interpretation of them in that Christianity represented a shift of emphasis away from the Torah towards the prophets. Christianity began its career as a religion which claimed that the end of the times, the last age, had arrived, and that Jesus the Messiah had come to usher in this end. It began in an atmosphere of eschatological, indeed apocalyptic, expectation. A great part of its claims lay in proving, or in attempting to prove, that it was in fulfilment of prophecy that, not merely the Messiah, but this Messiah, Jesus, had come, that the scriptures, if properly read, were full of veiled hints and indications as well as open and direct predictions of his eventual advent. This no doubt formed the staple of Paul's preaching in the synagogues of the dispersion. Indeed the compiling of proof-texts to show that all incidents of Christ's career, from his birth, through his ministry, arrest, trial, and execution, to the resurrection were predicted in the Jewish scriptures, along with several details of the church's life, was the first form that Christian doctrine took.

Christians did not find it very difficult to carry out this deciphering or re-interpreting process on the historical narratives, on the prophetic writings and on the wisdom literature, including the psalms, because they were able to take over techniques of interpretation already in familiar use in Judaism. But the interpretation of the Law in a Christological sense was a more difficult and speculative business, and its results were less convincing and less open to popular exposition. The tortuous allegorizations of the author of the *Epistle to Barnabas,* of Justin Martyr in his *Dialogue with Trypho,* of Origen in his

Homilies on Leviticus can have meant little to the ordinary Christian. The existing Jewish tradition of allegorization and harmonisation of the Torah was of little assistance, because it was directed towards making the varied and heterogeneous ordinances of the Pentateuch into a workable code to direct the lives of Jewish communities throughout the Roman Empire and beyond it, and this had no relevance for Christians after the 1st century.

The *Letter to Flora* by the gnostic Ptolemy, written in the middle of the 2nd century, shows that the interpretation of the law books was a matter of concern to Christians. It was easy enough to incorporate the moral commandments and regulations in a code of Christian ethics, its directions about relations between the sexes and family life and so on. We can see this happening in the rudimentary beginnings of canon law, in the Canons of Gregory Theodorus in the second half of the 3rd century, in the canons of the early councils at the turn of the 3rd to the 4th century, and in the Canonical Letters of Basil of Caesarea in the second half of the 4th century. But this still left a large mass of legislative material connected with the cult of the Jewish temple which could not be allegorized conveniently, could not be simply jettisoned, and yet seemed irrelevant to any particular Christian concern. But if most, or even some, of this material could be applied to the clergy of the Christian church, then the Law could take on a new meaning, indeed much of the cultic apparatus and legislation of the old dispensation could be adapted to the new. To begin to regard bishops as high priests was to open a door to the enhancement of the significance of the Christian clergy and to the possibility of, so to speak, reclaiming a substantial part of the wastelands of the Old Testament. We can see the appeal that this possibility must have had. Its more remote consequences can only have been hidden from the Christians of the 3rd century.

Another contributing force to this movement for developing a Christian priesthood must have been the example of pagan religion. It would be quite untrue to say that the Christian church borrowed wholesale from paganism during the pre-Constantinian period (or indeed very heavily even after that period). The church during these centuries was spending much of its time and energy waging war against paganism.

43

Because of their refusal to make any compromises with pagan religions practices and their sustained polemic against all forms of pagan cult, and particularly against cultic sacrifice, Christians were stigmatized as atheists and Christianity as an atheist religion. When Alexander the Prophet set up a highly successful and lucrative cult of Apollo under the form of a serpent in the small Asian town of Abounoteichos in the 2nd century, during the annual festival of the god, a crier went round, according to Lucian (who devoted a whole work to *Alexander the False Prophet*), excluding Epicureans and Christians on the ground that they were atheists. It was forbidden to Christians to enter a temple; Gregory of Nazianzus records with pride that his mother never even looked at a pagan temple. To take any part at all in pagan worship was considered a serious sin.

It is therefore in the last degree unlikely that Christians would either consciously or unconsciously borrow any feature at all from pagan worship, especially when the Roman government which was their chief enemy and which was liable at any time to prosecute them for professing the name of Christian was an official supporter and patron of many pagan cults. But it is quite probable that the title of high priest was adopted partly at least in emulation of pagan religion. After all, the titles of Christian ministers of religion, bishops, priests and deacons, were not hallowed by any special associations with either the Old Testament or with the very earliest days of Christianity. One can imagine a Christian during his conversation with a pagan neighbour (and in spite of the gloomy warnings of Tertullian Christians did make friends with their pagan neighbours) being asked in an amicable spirit what was the leader of his cult called. 'We have a high priest of our cult,' the pagan might say; 'What is the leader of your cult called?' To this the Christian could only reply lamely, 'Ours is called an inspector.'

The *archiereus* in the Greek-speaking east and *sacerdos* in the Latin-speaking west, if his cult was an important one, could be an important and influential figure in the local community. Several of the major cities of the east, such as Alexandria, Antioch and Ephesus, had a chief priest whose function was to co-ordinate the cults of the city, so that they would not, for instance, hold major festivals at the same time. He might well be the priest of the cult of the genius of the emperor and part of his task would be to see that each cult as far as possible adjusted itself to the business of giving proper respect to the imperial family. A chief priest, whether he was *archiereus* of the city or not, would probably be a person who stood high in social esteem and who walked with the great and powerful. Christians in the 3rd century may well have perceived the possibility of winning increased social esteem and standing for their clergy by following the inviting Old Testament precedent and calling them high priests and priests. We have already seen (page 40) that there is a hint of this in one passage in the *Didascalia Apostolorum*.

A final factor in preparing for the emergence of a Christian priesthood was the lengthening gulf between the church and Judaism. As long as the Christian church had to struggle, first to maintain itself as a distinct sect within Judaism and then to realize its identity as a separate religion from Judaism and in rivalry to it, the appearance of a Christian priesthood would have been impossible. An official priesthood, a regularly maintained sacrificial cult, a hierarchy—these were just the sort of things which characterised Judaism and from which Christianity wished to distinguish itself. And there is plenty of evidence that the emphasizing of this distinction formed one of the themes of early Christian literature. But by the year 200 Judaism offered no serious threat and little serious rivalry to Christianity. There were places, such as Syriac-speaking parts of Syria and Mesopotamia and Persia, where Judaism offered a threat to Christianity. Christian propaganda against the Jews was maintained, as Cyprian's *Testimonia ad Quirinum vel Adversus Iudaeos* (which consists largely of previously existing material) shows.

Origen was always conscious of the Jews as a point of view existing in the territory between the church and paganism, and indeed himself cultivated friendship with some Jewish scholars and learnt from them. But by and large contemporary Judaism had faded from the foreground of Christian thought. Jewish vocabulary, formulae, prayers, images and traditions were embedded in much Christian thought and practice, but by 200 Christianity no longer lived in a Jewish milieu nor was

45

preoccupied with Jewish concerns. The cult carried on in the Jewish temple which was a living reality in the time of Jesus and Paul was now no more than a distant memory; Judaism no longer embodied a sacrificial cult. It was therefore possible by the year 200 to contemplate treating Christian clergy as if they were Christianised versions of Old Testament clergy and to apply Old Testament terms of cultic sacrificial priesthood to their activity without a sense of incongruousness or a fear of falling back into Judaism. Whether this was a proper, healthy and satisfactory development remains to be seen.

Eucharistic Offering in the Early Church

Before we consider the major development of the concept of Christian priesthood represented by the work of Cyprian, we must turn our attention to another subject which at this point contributes significantly to the doctrine of priesthood, and that is the subject of eucharistic offering.

From a very early period Christian writers had claimed that in distinction from both Judaism and paganism, the Christian cult offered to God not the material offerings of animal or vegetable sacrifices, but a 'pure offering', invoking regularly the text of Malachi 1:11, 'For from the rising of the sun to its setting my name is great among the nations, and in every place incense is offered in my name, and a pure offering, for my name is great among the nations, says the Lord of hosts.' This, they claimed, was a prediction by the inspired prophet of the coming of Christianity which would spread among the nations, substituting for the polluted offering of Judaism (Mal. 1:12) and the demon-inspired sacrifices of paganism the 'pure offering'. What the 'pure offering' meant was a pure heart, a pure conscience, a pure mind, and also prayer, praise and thanksgiving. Writer after writer could be quoted as authorities for this doctrine (for details see my 'Eucharistic Offering in the Pre-Nicene Fathers', pages 75–78) which is indeed one of the commonplaces of early Christian literature, and continues to be repeated regularly by almost every writer up to Eusebius of Caesarea in the 4th century, even by those writers who also expound a different doctrine of offering connected with the eucharist.

46

The doctrine of the 'pure offering' must originally have had no connection with the eucharist. It can be found in germ in Paul's words at Romans 12:1, 'I appeal to you therefore, brethren, by the mercies of God, to present your bodies as a living sacrifice, holy and acceptable to God, which is your spiritual worship'. The doctrine of the 'pure offering' need not be linked with the eucharist and in many writers is advanced in contexts which are not eucharistic. But it can be associated with the eucharist because in this service, the participants offer themselves to God. The *Didache* does so in a well-known passage, directly appealing to Malachi 1:11 (*Did.* 14.1,2):

> On the Lord's Day come together, break bread and hold eucharist, after confessing your transgressions that your sacrifice (*thysia*) may be pure; but let none who has a quarrel with his fellow join in your meeting until they be reconciled, that your sacrifice (*thysia*) be not defiled.

The sacrific must be the Christian's offering of himself. It is possible that the same eucharistic reference is intended in the words of Hermas' *Shepherd*, 'your sacrifice (*thysia*) will be acceptable with God' (*Similitudes* V.3 (56.8)).

Side by side with this doctrine of the 'pure offering' there grew up in the early church another doctrine of offering, associated from the beginning with the eucharist. It occurs in its earliest known form in 1 Clement, where the duty of the presbyters is said to be not only to exercise pastoral care over the Christian community but also 'to present the gifts' (*prospherein ta dōra*), i.e. to present the bread and the wine in the eucharist so that they shall be blessed by God (44,4). Justin reproduces the same idea, but he actually blends and combines it with the thought of the 'pure offering', taking the passage in Malachi as a prediction both of the offering of prayers and thanksgiving and also of the presentation before God of bread and wine, both types of offering being combined in the eucharistic rite (*Dialogue* 41.1–3; *Apology* 65:3;67:5). He virtually identifies the eucharistised bread and wine with the body and blood of Christ (*Apology* 67). He does not directly connect the offering of the bread and wine with the action of the celebrant but with that of the congregation when they present the elements to be blessed by God at the prayer of the celebrant. Significant though this language may appear to us in view of later developments in eucharistic doctrine, Justin has not moved, as far as a doctrine of offering is concerned, significantly further than 1 Clement. The Christian congregation gathers to make prayer and thanksgiving to God, and to present to God the gifts of bread and wine for him to bless.

The doctrine of eucharistic offering in Irenaeus does not advance much beyond this point, except that he has an idea peculiar to himself and not developed later by others that the bread and the wine represent the first fruits of God's own creation which men offer back to God (*Adv. Haer.* IV.29.5). This doctrine need not detain us here. In general, Irenaeus' teaching is that Christians offer to God on the one hand praise and thanksgiving (the 'pure offering') and on the other hand bread and wine to be transformed by God into the body and blood of Christ so that men can have communion with Christ; and he stresses that God never demanded of anybody, Jews or Gentiles, a better sacrifice than a pure heart and a humble mind (IV.29.1–4). It is not the offering that matters but the sincerity and single heart of the offerer (IV.31.2), and our offering should express our gratitude, faith, hope and love (IV.31.3). The gifts which we offer in the eucharist are not needed by God, but it is fitting that we should show our gratitude to him in this way (IV.31.1). When the bread receives the invocation it ceases to be ordinary bread but is 'eucharist consisting of two things, earthly and heavenly' (IV.31.4). Just as the word directed the people under the old covenant to make offerings so that they should learn to serve God, so 'he wishes us also to offer a gift at the altar frequently and unceasingly' (IV.31.5). Though the 'realistic' doctrine of the consecrated elements is markedly present in Irenaeus' thought, he makes no special connection at all between the celebrant and the elements, but seems, like Justin, to regard them as virtually offered by the people. His almost apologetic tone in speaking of the idea that men should offer anything to God shows how far he is from the thought that the celebrant offers Christ in the eucharist.

Tertullian is as stout an exponent of the doctrine of the 'pure offering' as anybody (e.g. *Apologeticus* 30.5(71); *Adv. Marcionem* II.22.3; III.22.6; IV.1.8,35.11; *Adv. Judaeos* V.5–7.) One striking example (*De Oratione* 28.3,4) will suffice for all:

We are the true worshippers and the true priests who sacrifice in the spirit prayer as a suitable and acceptable sacrifice (*hostiam*) of God, which of course he demanded, which he foresaw for himself. We are bound to offer at God's altar this prayer, dedicated with all the heart, nourished by faith, protected by truth, sincere in its singleheartedness, pure in its chastity, crowned by love and accompanied by good actions along with psalms and hymns —and it gains everything for us from God.

As in the case of Irenaeus, this doctrine can coexist along with a markedly 'realistic' doctrine of the nature of the consecrated elements (e.g. *Ad. Marc.* IV.40.3;V.8.3.). We have seen already (page 38) that Tertullian uses the word *offerre* (to offer) of the celebrant at the eucharist; he also frequently uses the term *oblatio* (offering) and *sacrificium* (sacrifice) of the rite (references in 'Eucharistic Offering,' page 83). But he explains carefully that this offering and sacrifice are an offering and sacrifice only of prayers; 'your sacrifice shall ascend' means that your prayer shall mount up (*De Ex. Cast.*, 11.2), and he can use the expression 'not however without sacrifice which is a soul mortified by fasts' (*De Ieiun. ad Psych.*, 16:1). And he gives no sign of connecting the eucharist with Christ's sacrifice. We have seen already that he describes clergy as priests but he does not significantly connect this with the function of the clergy in the eucharist. In short, Tertullian supplies much of the vocabulary but little of the theology of later eucharistic doctrine.

A certain development of eucharistic doctrine is evident both in Hippolytus and in the *Didascalia Apostolorum*, though neither make any striking alteration. There is one slight indication of the idea of the 'pure offering' in Hippolytus' *Apostolic Tradition* (3). The bread and wine are described more than once as 'the offering' (*prosphora*), and the final part of the model prayer for the bishop to make in the eucharist includes the words 'we offer to thee the bread and the cup making eucharist to thee' (4). The prayer for the Holy Spirit in the eucharist makes no mention of a conversion of the elements, but in the passage governing the presentation of the bread and the wine by the deacons to the bishop it is said (as far as we make out from an uncertain text, here reconstructed by Botte (21, pages 54 and 55), that the bishop will give thanks over the bread that

49

it may become the representation (*antitypos*) of the body of Christ and over the cup of wine, that it may become the likeness (*homoiōma*) of the blood of Christ, and in another passage the eucharist is directly referred to as the body of Christ while the cup is called the antitype of the blood of Christ (37, 38). Apparently at no time in the *Apostolic Tradition* is the eucharistic table called an altar. As with Tertullian, no significant connection is made between the celebrant and the effect of the prayer upon the elements. The *Didascalia* has a much more prominent doctrine of the 'pure offering', which appears in the same passage as one which describes the bishop as a high priest (IX.86, where there is a passage rejecting all sacrifices):

> Instead of the sacrifices which then were, offer now prayers and petitions and thanksgivings. Then were first fruits and tithes and part-offerings and gifts, but today the oblations which are offered through the bishop to the Lord God. For they are your high priests.

The author calls widows and orphans 'the altar of Christ' (XVII.154; XVIII.156), and he interprets the text Matthew 5:23 ('If thou offer thy gift upon the altar . . .') so that the gift means 'our prayer and our eucharist' (XI.116), and this passage, along with another (XI.117), echoes the sentiment (see page 47) which we have already found in the *Didache* (which is certainly one of the sources of the *Didascalia*) in warning its hearers not to defile the offering by bad behaviour. Finally it is worth noting that the *Didascalia* uses language of the consecrated elements reminiscent of the language of both Hippolytus and of Irenaeus: 'Offer an acceptable eucharist, the likeness of the royal body of Christ. . . pure bread that is made with fire and sanctified by invocations' (XXVI.252); the original of the word translated 'likeness' here was probably *antitypos*. Once again we note that though the author's language shows some advance in eucharistic doctrine he has not made any significant connection between the celebrant and the consecrated elements.

The Christian platonists of Alexandria, Clement and Origen, reproduce for the most part the traditional ideas both of priesthood and of eucharistic offering, though Origen at least has his own peculiar interpretation of both, as he had of

50

the priesthood of all believers (see above page 30). There is no sign of the practice of calling Christian clergy priests in Clement of Alexandria, and this fact is confirmation of the conclusion that the practice only arose at the beginning of the 3rd century. The true priest or high priest, according to Clement, is the morally and spiritually advanced Christian, the gnostic (*Stromateis* IV.25 [158.1] V.6 [39.3–4], V.11.7 [36.2]). But Origen, writing a generation later, calls bishops and presbyters high priests and priests throughout his works without embarrassment as an accepted practice, and can compare bishops to the high priests of the Jewish cult (for the references see 'Eucharistic Offering' page 188). Clement has a full testimony to the doctrine of the 'pure offering' without specifically linking it to the eucharist (for instances see 'Eucharistic Offering' page 87). 'And indeed the sacrifice of the church is the Word sent up as incense by holy souls while all their intention is manifested to God along with the sacrifice' (*Stromateis* VII.6.32) is one of his most striking expressions of the concept. The sacrifices of the Christian gnostic 'are prayers and praises and intercessions and psalms and hymns before the shrine of the scriptures' (*Strom.* VII.7.48). The word altar (*thysiasterion*) means the gathering on earth of those who are devoted to prayer united in a common voice and mind (*Strom.* VII.5.3). He uses *prosphora* (offering) of the eucharist, but does not draw any doctrine out of the bishop's or priest's capacity to celebrate the eucharist.

Origen's doctrine of the 'pure offering' is quite conventional, and can be gathered from many parts of his work (for references see 'Eucharistic Offering' page 87). Christians have no temples or altars because 'our altars are the mind of each righteous man from which true and intelligible incense with a sweet savour is sent up, prayers from a true conscience' (*Contra Celsum* VIII.17). God needs nothing: Christians have nothing to do with material sacrifices. He reproduces readily the 'realist' account of the consecrated elements which the church of his day held, and can describe how carefully Christians refrain from dropping even a crumb of the eucharistic bread when the receive 'the body of the Lord' (*Homily on Exodus* 13:3 (PG 12:389–90)). In another passage he writes (*Contra Celsum* VIII.33):

51

But we give thanks to the Creator of the Universe and eat the loaves that are presented with thanksgiving and prayer over the gifts, so that by the prayer they become a certain holy body which sanctifies those who partake of it with a pure intention.

Origen has, as has already been indicated, his own idiosyncratic interpretation of the eucharist (as of baptism) and of the narratives of the institution of the eucharist, arising out of his remarkable synthesis of platonism and Christianity, which is irrelevant to our purpose here. But, as the texts just quoted suggest, he inherited and endorsed much the same eucharistic doctrine as that of Irenaeus and of Tertullian: the church presents or offers the gifts of bread and wine in the eucharist for God to bless in order that Christians may communicate. He does not connect the priesthood which he ascribes to Christian clergy in any ways specifically with their celebration of the eucharist.

Cyprian

As we now move on to consider how these various strands of doctrine combine to form a new and striking concept of priesthood in the work of Cyprian of Carthage, it is as well to remind ourselves of what had and what had not been achieved before Cyprian came on the scene. The doctrine of the 'pure offering' which entailed the rejection of any material form of offering to God made by Christians and above all of any animal sacrifices, which included the scornful disparagement of material altars and incense and all other such apparatus, which condemned the Jewish and derided the pagan form of sacrificial rite, had been echoed and reproduced with a virtual unanimity for two centuries at least. Bishops and presbyters had indeed been called high priests and priests, but not because they celebrated the eucharist or offered anything to God except prayers and praises and pure hearts and consciences. The words offer and offering had been used familiarly of the eucharist but still with the thought that it was the people who offered through the celebrant; and what was offered was thought of, at the most extreme, as the antitype or likeness of the body and blood of Christ. Nobody had gone as far as to say that either the people or the celebrant offered Christ himself. And if the clergy were called priests this priesthood was still not defined in terms of a sacrificial cult.

If any attempt was made to determine why Christian priests were priests, it was in terms either of representing the priestly ministry of Christ or of exercising a power to forgive sins. But on the whole the practice of calling bishops and presbyters priests had not brought any particular theology with it, any more than earlier the titles of bishop, presbyter and deacon had brought a theology with them. There were, in short, a number of ingredients for a new doctrine of priesthood present: a concept of offering; a concept of the conversion of bread and wine into the body and blood of Christ; the names priest and high priest. But these ingredients had not yet been put together to form the highly intoxicating brew which Cyprian was to produce.

Cyprian was in some ways an exception among the writers of literature of the first three centuries. He certainly was a well educated man. He had had an exceptionally good education in the school of the *rhetor* and perhaps also as a professional lawyer. He could write a distinctive, graceful, easy, charming Latin style. And he was a man of outstanding ability. He was a great administrator; he was a clearheaded man of strong mind who did not find it difficult to make important decisions. He was a natural leader who could not help influencing those with whom he came in contact. And he must have been a persuasive and attractive person also towards those with whom he talked and with whom he corresponded. He had a peculiarly Roman *gravitas* and both physical and moral courage. All these virtues and talents equipped him to become an outstanding Christian figure within a surprisingly short time of his conversion to Christianity.

But these qualities and capacities are in some respects a handicap when their possessor is required to be a theologian if he has not had sufficient theological education. They give him confidence without judgment. They tempt him to take illegitimate short cuts. They induce him to drive forward vigorously on a theological journey whose end he is not sufficiently qualified to foresee. He cannot envisage the dangers, the ambiguities and compromising consequences of the

53

course upon which he resolutely embarks. To him all is splendidly simple. Scripture, tradition, reason, are all so much plastic material for him to use in the argument which he sees all too clearly leading in the direction to which he is determined it shall go. Just such a man was Cyprian.

He was one of those men of action who make doctrine as successful generals make strategy, like Hildebrand, like General Booth. He can have had little theological education. No doubt the two or at most three years that elapsed between his conversion to Christianity and his being elected bishop of Carthage were spent by him in intensive study. He knew the Latin Bible well. He had read and valued the works of Tertullian. But there can have been little time for further theological formation. We have no reason for thinking that the African church had many well equipped theologians who could have given him an effective commando course in their discipline. In his *Testimonia*, written before he became bishop, he certainly used the work of some other author, without apparently perceiving that on several points it diverged notably from ideas which he already held, or at least was shortly to hold. With this meagre equipment he set forth on his career as a bishop, a career which was to make him a great leader, a famous martyr, and a father of the church whose doctrine of priesthood was to form the thinking of the western church upon that subject for well over a thousand years.

In the first place, Cyprian believes that bishops have been directly instituted by Christ in that Christ consecrated the twelve apostles as bishops and they in their turn consecrated their successors as bishops, and so by a succession of bishops the bishops of Cyprian's own day bear Christ's authority by a line of authority virtually independent of the rest of the church. For him the apostles are the models for a bishop to follow, and Peter was given a primacy among them in order to impress on them the indispensable necessity for unity in the church. Next, all bishops are priests, on the analogy of the priests of the Old Testament. He applies the word *sacerdotes* to presbyters as well as to bishops (e.g. *Letters* 1.1.7), and he takes the sacerdotal status of clergy more seriously than any previous writer. Because they are priests, clergy are sacrosanct. A deacon who has attacked Rogatianus, a bishop, is liable to the

54

punishment of death for sacrilege (*Letters* III.1.1,2):

> And that we may be sure that this utterance of God (Deut. 17:12,13) proceeded from his authentic and highest divine authority, in order to honour and defend his priests, when three of the assistants, Korah, Dathan and Abiram, dared to raise their authority against Aaron the priest and make themselves equal with the priest placed over them, they were swallowed and devoured by an abyss in the ground and immediately paid the penalty of their sacrilegious presumption.

Many other passages could be adduced in the same vein throughout Cyprian's correspondence. And Cyprian, to emphasize the priestly character of the clergy, closely connects the altar and the priesthood:

> God is one and Christ is one and one chair has been founded on Peter by the Lord's utterance. Another altar cannot be set up nor a new priesthood come into being save the one altar and the one priesthood. (*Letters* 43.5.2)

This close association of priesthood with the celebration of the eucharist represents a new development in the theology of the Christian priesthood.

Cyprian's doctrine of eucharistic offering enhances and develops even further the doctrine concerning priesthood. He witnesses, indeed, to the vigorous survival of the old doctrine of the 'pure offering' alongside new ideas about offering. He inherited in the material which he took over in the *Testimonia* several expositions of the 'pure offering' (*Test.* I.16), and also a doctrine of the ministry which was not sacerdotal (III.111 and 85), and a concept of eucharistic offering which was the conventional teaching that in the eucharist men offer gifts to God and the gifts must not be defiled by wicked conduct (I.22 (citing Ecclesiasticus 34:19(23)) and II.2). But elsewhere, even in his latest works, Cyprian repeats the doctrine of the 'pure offering' which he plainly regarded as not inconsistent with his other doctrines (*De Dom. Orat.* 23,33; *Letters* 76.3.1,2). Even in his 63rd letter he labours to show that the people are offered to Christ along with the bread and the wine:

> For because Christ was bearing all of us in that he was bearing our sins, we see that in the water (i.e. the water mixed with the wine at

55

the eucharist) the people is signified, but in the wine the blood of Christ. But when water is mixed with wine in the chalice the people is united with Christ and the company of believers is linked and joined with him in whom it believes. . . . So nothing can separate from Christ a people which is faithfully and firmly in the church and perseveres in its beliefs so as to prevent it always cleaving to him and its undivided love continuing. . . . For if anyone offers wine only, it begins to be Christ without us. But if there is only water, the people begins to be there without Christ. But when each is mixed and combined with the other in an indiscriminate combination then the spiritual and heavenly mystery is completed. (*Letters* 63.13.1–3)

There can be no doubt that Cyprian believes that the eucharist is an offering of the people themselves to God, but it is already evident that his eucharistic doctrine goes much further than this.

This 63rd letter is the place where Cyprian expounds his views about the eucharist most fully; we can find nothing like so open an expression of his ideas on the subject elsewhere. But that is a matter of chance; we have no reason to assume that this one letter does not represent his characteristic doctrine. All his letters, with a very few exceptions, were called forth by the accidents and circumstances of the time in which they were written; this letter to Caecilius, apparently a fellow bishop, was written in all probability because Cyprian had heard that some people were celebrating the eucharist either with wine unmixed with water or even with water alone apart from wine. It calls forth from him a long and carefully considered exposition of eucharistic doctrine.

His basic conviction is that bishops when they celebrate must do what Christ did when at the last supper he celebrated the first eucharist (63:1.1). In the eucharist the cup is offered in commemoration of Christ and in this cup is 'his body by which we were redeemed and quickened' (2.1.2). Christ offered his body and blood as a sacrifice for us (4.1.). The logical consequence is clear:

It is clear that the blood of Christ is not offered if the wine is not in the cup nor the Lord's sacrifice celebrated with a valid consecration unless our offering and sacrifice corresponds to the passion (9.3).

56

What this correspondence to the passion means is made clear a little later in the letter:

> For if Christ Jesus our Lord and God is himself the high priest of God the Father and first offered himself as a sacrifice to the Father and ordered that this should be done in commemoration of him then of course that priest functions rightly in the place of Christ who imitates what Christ did and offers in the church the full and true sacrifice, if he so begins to offer according to what he sees Christ himself to have offered (14.4).

And towards the end of the letter Cyprian firmly links this doctrine with the passion once again:

> And because we mention his passion in all our sacrifices, for the passion of the Lord is the sacrifice we offer, we ought to do nothing else than what he did. For the Bible says that as often as we offer the cup in the commemoration of the Lord and his passion we do that which it is certain that the Lord has done (17.1).

In short, Cyprian's doctrine of eucharistic offering is that when the priest (i.e. the bishop, though he would no doubt apply the same doctrine to the presbyter) offers the bread and the wine in the eucharist he is doing precisely what Christ did, either at the last supper or in his whole redemptive activity; he is offering Christ's body and blood, the identical physical organism which was his when he walked the lanes of Galilee and the streets of Jerusalem, as a sacrifice in order to expiate the sins of the whole world, or, to put the matter in another way, he is offering the passion of Christ as a sacrifice to God, just as Christ offered himself as a sacrifice to God, and at the same time the people are, through the priest, offering themselves to God. It is worth noting that Cyprian invokes the high-priesthood of Christ to ground his doctrine of the priesthood of the clergy.

In this doctrine Cyprian has put together all existing elements of a doctrine of eucharistic offering into a new synthesis pregnant with important consequences for the doctrine of the eucharist and the doctrine of the priesthood. What is new in this is firstly, the close linking of the priestly character of the ministry with its function in celebrating the eucharist, and particularly in offering a sacrifice, not just of prayer and praise, not just of the hearts and consciences of the congregation, but

57

of the literal body and blood of Christ. Nobody had shown an inclination to do this before, and in this linking of priesthood and eucharistic offering of this sort Cyprian has taken a long stride towards defining Christian priesthood in terms of a sacrificial cult.

Secondly, Cyprian has imported a new emphasis in linking the priestly activity of the clergy in the eucharist with the passion and death of Christ, so as to say that they actually offer Christ's passion when they celebrate. This again, curiously enough, nobody else had hitherto shown any strong desire to do. The eucharist had of course been linked with the death of Christ; it could hardly be otherwise. But neither the doctrine of offering nor the thought of the clergy as priests had been associated with Christ's death. The offering hitherto had been the offering made by men, the offering of praise, or of themselves, or of the bread and wine for God to bless. Now a new step has been taken: the bishop as priest offers the consecrated elements which have become Christ's body and blood, and become so in a quite unqualified way, with no concession given to an antitype or likeness. Irenaeus' hesitation about the thought that man could offer anything to God in any circumstances has become a confident declaration that the priest offers Christ and Christ's sacrifice to God.

It is Cyprian's confidence that perhaps impresses the student more unfavourably than anything else about his doctrine of priesthood and eucharistic offering. It is the same confidence as that with which he opposed Stephen bishop of Rome on the subject of the re-baptism of heretics. He was quite certain that scripture (which is in fact wholly silent upon the subject) was on his side here, that *veritas* (truth) must prevail against mere *consuetudo* (custom). So here he surges confidently forward into an exposition of priesthood and eucharistic offering which is indeed to contribute most of its elements to the doctrine of the medieval western church upon the subject, but which is also ultimately to transform the Christian ministry as it was in the 3rd century out of all recognition and lead to the break up of the unity of the western church in the 16th century. We must not heap all the responsibility of the later doctrine of priesthood on Cyprian, because, as we shall see, he was only anticipating a not dissimilar doctrine which

58

was to develop a century later in the eastern church, but he achieved in one hasty leap what was to be reached only gradually and tentatively by the more cautious and judicious theologians of the east. A church which began by contemptuously rejecting all forms of sacrifice except the most immaterial has come perilously near to instituting its own sacrificial cult, with altars and priests who offer sacrifices which, whatever allowance we make for the imprecision of piety or the exaggeration of rhetoric, cannot be described as wholly immaterial or spiritual.

Lactantius and Eusebius

Cyprian's example, his authority, certainly had a profound influence on the doctrine of priesthood of the western church, and we can see his ideas and vocabulary reproduced not long after his death in more than one writer (see 'Eucharistic Offering', page 91). But that his ideas did not penetrate everywhere in the world of Latin-speaking Christianity is shown by the example of Lactantius who, writing in Latin in the opening years of the 4th century, shows no influence from Cyprian at all; on the contrary, his ideas seem in some respects to be in total contradiction to those of Cyprian. He of course describes Christian clergy as priests (*sacerdotes*); this was a normal and conventional term for them in his day. But his doctrine of the 'pure offering' is so extreme as to leave virtually no room for any other form of offering, and if taken seriously it would apparently render any sort of public or communal cult by Christians unnecessary. He contrasts the sacrifices of pagans with those of Christians. The Christian cult is pure and refined, unlike the coarse and disgusting sacrifices of paganism 'because it has the mind itself as a sacrifice' (*Divine Institutes* V.19.30). He can call the eucharist a *sacrificium*, but only, as far as one can see, because it consists of this 'pure offering'. 'This is the true cult', he says, 'in which the mind of the worshippers offers itself as a spotless victim to God' (*Div. Inst.* VI.2.13). Sacrifice can also be defined as works of mercy, ransoming prisoners, supporting the poor, burying the dead (*Div. Inst.* VI.12.39–41). And he uses these emphatic words towards the end of the 6th book of the *Divine Institutes*:

Whoever therefore obeys all these heavenly commands is a wor-
shipper of the true God, whose sacrifices are gentleness of mind
and an innocent life and good actions. Whoever manifests all
these, sacrifices as often he performs any good and pious act. For
God does not want a victim consisting of a dumb animal nor its
death nor its blood, but that of a man and his life. . . . And so there
is placed on the altar of God, which is really the Great Altar and
which cannot be defiled because it is situated in man's heart,
righteousness, patience, faith, innocence, chastity, temperance.
(*Div. Inst.* VI.24, 27–29)

In the course of these last few chapters of the 6th book of the
Divine Institutes he distinguishes between the temporary gift
(*donum*) given to God and the eternal sacrifice. We might here
expect a distinction between the bread and wine supplied by
men and Christ's sacrifice offered to God. But we would be
disappointed: gift means integrity of mind, sacrifice praise and
hymnody (25.7). Sacrifice on our part can only consist of
blessing, made by words. There is no need for a temple in this
worship; it can just as well be given at home: 'in fact each man
has God always consecrated in his heart because he is the
Temple of God' (25.16). In this radical doctrine of offering
there is no room at all for a priest offering the sacrifice of Christ
to God.

In the eastern church the doctrine of priesthood in connection with eucharistic sacrifice did not advance as quickly as it
did among those writers who were influenced by Cyprian in
the west. Methodius of Olympus, writing in Greek in the early
years of the 4th century, appears, as far as we can make out
from the text which survives only in an Old Slavonic translation, to distinguish between the eucharistic elements and 'the
offering of the mind, a rational sacrifice, spiritual gifts' (*De
Resurrectione* III.23(472)).

At about the same time Eusebius of Caesarea, the ecclesiastical historian, was expounding in his works a carefully
thought out account of eucharistic sacrifice which fell far short
of the lengths that Cyprian was to go in this respect. Eusebius
fully endorses the doctrine of the 'pure sacrifice', that is the
offering of a pure mind and of good actions and prayers (for
references see 'Eucharistic Offering', pages 93–94). At one
place he says, in words reminiscent of Lactantius, that each
60

man now offers, not in Jerusalem, nor with animal and bloody sacrifice, but 'at home and in his own place the unbloody and pure worship in spirit and in truth' (*Demonstratio Evangelica* I.6.57(32); cf 65(33) and *Vita Constantini* 1.48). But he also treats the subject of eucharistic sacrifice in its strict sense, in the 10th chapter of the first book of his *Demonstratio Evangelica* (sections 1–38). Christ made the final and effective sacrifice, superseding all others (14–17(45)), and this is what Christians commemorate, 'celebrating daily the memorial of his body and his blood' (18(46)). Christ offered his human nature to God (23(47)) and left us a memorial to offer continually to God 'instead of a sacrifice' (25(47)). We have received the command 'to celebrate a memorial of this sacrifice at a table through symbols of his body and of his saving blood according to the ordinances of new covenant' (28(47)). The 'holy sacrifices of Christ's table' are those in which we offer 'bloodless and reasonable sacrifices appropriate to him through all our lives to the God of all' through Christ our high priest (29(48)).

Not long after Eusebius introduces the idea of the 'pure offering', the sacrifice of praise and of the contrite spirit and of prayer (36, 37(49)). And he summarizes his doctrine in these words (38(49)):

> Therefore we both sacrifice and burn incense: on the one hand we celebrate the memorial of the great sacrifice according to the mysteries handed down to us by him, and we proffer thanksgiving for our salvation through pious hymns and prayers to God; on the other hand we dedicate ourselves to him alone and to his high-priestly Word, devoted in body and soul.

In a later book of the same work Eusebius returns briefly to the subject (V.3.19.222):

> First our Saviour and Lord himself, then all priests (*hiereis*) throughout all nations deriving from him perform their spiritual cultic service (*hierourgia*) according to the Church's regulations and accomplish their mysterious rites of his body and of his saving blood with wine and bread.

Eusebius in short has no objection to calling clergy priests, and does so constantly throughout his voluminous writings, but he does not define their function in purely cultic terms nor particularly stress their action in the eucharist. In the majority of the quotations given above his 'we' denotes the Christian people as a whole. The priestly activity of both people and priests is based on Christ's priesthood, which it expresses. He does not conceive of priests offering Christ in the eucharist. The sacrifice offered is basically the traditional 'pure offering', but he does connect the action of the people and priest in the eucharist with Christ's death. They celebrate the memorial of Christ's sacrificial death through the symbols of bread and wine, elements symbolic of his body and his blood. Eusebius regularly reproduces in his works the 'realistic' account of the consecrated elements in the eucharist which was universal in the church of his day. But he does not allow this doctrine to push him into saying that the priest offers Christ's body and blood to God in the eucharist. He shows his prudence as a theologian in recognizing how ill this idea would assort with the traditional doctrine of the 'pure offering'.

The Fourth Century

Other forces were, however, working in the east as well as in the west towards the development of a much stronger doctrine of priesthood. The treatment of the church by the Emperor Constantine had ultimately a marked influence upon the church's doctrine as well as upon its worldly situation and prospects. In the first place it meant that in the west from 313 and in the east from 325 onwards Christianity, instead of being a proscribed religion struggling for survival against a powerful autocratic government, found itself basking in the sun of imperial patronage, and loaded with money, privileges and responsibilities. It became an advantage instead of a handicap for ambitious and worldly and powerful people to become Christians. To be numbered among the clergy was, for a short time at least before the sacred treasury realized how expensive a privilege it had granted, to escape the necessity of paying a tax which was as onerous and as crippling as the British middle classes find income tax today. It is easy to imagine how many people suddenly wanted to become Christians, and how many middle-class *curiales* (people liable to be made compulsory town councillors) experienced a sudden vocation to holy orders.

In the face of a serious threat to the church's authenticity and integrity, a threat of the dilution of its standards and the profanation of its sacraments, the clergy very naturally reacted by making the sacraments deliberately difficult of access. They encouraged catechumens who were in civil or military office not to be baptized until they had left the imperial service. They enacted a rule, for instance, that nobody should appear at church festivals in military dress. They emphasized more than ever the responsibility of becoming a baptized communicant. It must be remembered that for the church of the patristic period there was no gulf between the baptized and the communicants. If you were baptized, at whatever age, you automatically became a communicant. But we can trace in eucharistic doctrine as the 4th century advances a new emphasis, an emphasis upon the awefulness, the fearfulness, almost the danger, of the sacraments of baptism and of the eucharist, and especially of the latter. The altar is, so to speak, fenced by the use of awe-inspiring language about the eucharist; it is almost as if the consecrated elements were considered to be radio-active for all except those who were insulated against their dangerous power. And prominent among the insulated were of course the clergy. This fencing of the altar inevitably enhanced both their status and their power. They were the men who could control the dangerous mystery, who could enter the affected area unharmed.

Another result of the recognition of the church by the Roman government was the rapid and visible decline of paganism. Pagan cults had shown signs of decay before the 4th century, though not as many signs as Christian propagandists claimed. But now paganism in all its forms was manifestly dying. The Emperor Julian's attempt (361–2) to revive it, though it gave the Christians a bad fright and a deserved shock, only served in the end to show how little vitality there was left in the rival religions. And in fact the Christian church began to realize, from the end of the reign of Constantine (306–337) onwards that paganism no longer offered it serious competition. The result was that Christians now thought it safe to adopt the vocabulary of the pagan cults, and especially of the mystery religions, and began to do so with increasing freedom. Cyprian never called himself a *pontifex* (pontiff, a

63

pagan title) (though his biographer Pontius did), yet the word was in common use of Christian clergy by the 4th century. Titles such as *coryphaeus* (master of ceremonies) and *epoptes* (seer) and *hierophant* (Grand Master of the Lodge) were freely borrowed from the mystery religions for the clergy. The author, whether he was Cyril of Jerusalem or his successor John, who published addresses to catechumens not long after the middle of the 4th century called them *Mystagogical Catecheses;* and bishops would not have disdained the title of *mystagogue.* This tendency naturally reinforced the mystique of clergy as the controllers of the cultic mystery. It tended to make people define their functions and the nature of their office in terms of the cult, as the priests of the pagan cults and the administrators of the mystery religions had been defined.

Both these tendencies are illustrated in the last ancient text which we shall examine in the course of tracing the rise of the concept of a Christian priesthood in the ancient church, that is John Chrysostom's work *On the Priesthood (De Sacerdotio).* John wrote this work in 381, when he was a deacon, apparently in order to induce a friend of his called Basil to allow himself to become a candidate for the priesthood. Throughout he uses the words *hierosune* and *hiereus,* not presbyter, to denote the order which forms the subject of his work. At one point (II. 183) he describes the apostle Peter as 'the *coryphaeus* of the apostles'. In the 3rd book he occupies himself with describing the awe-inspiring nature of the priesthood. The Old Testament priesthood was terrifying enough, he says, with its array of bells and its breastplate and so on, but the New Testament priesthood is more awesome (III.4. 175–177):

> For when you see the Lord slaughtered and lying there and the priest standing over the sacrifice and interceding and everyone gleaming red with that precious blood, can you any longer imagine that you are among men and stand on earth, but do you not think that you have been translated to the heavens? (177.)

Next he compares the celebrant to Elijah calling down fire upon the offering on the altar (178). The Christian priest does not call down fire, but the Holy Spirit, and he intercedes, not that fire shall strike from heaven but 'that grace falling on the sacrifice may through it touch the souls of all and render them brighter than silver tested in the fire' (179). He describes this as 'a most terrifying performance' (*teletē*, a word taken from the rites of the mystery religions), and one that would consume all who witnessed it did not God's grace assist them (180).

A little later he calls attention to the immense power possessed by priests in administering penance and controlling the sacraments (III.5.181–189). 'And whatever the priests transact below God above endorses and the Master confirms the decision of his slaves' (183). If nobody can enter the kingdom of heaven except through baptism, administered by priests, and nobody can have eternal life except through eating the eucharistic elements, controlled by priests, they in fact control entry to heaven and hell (187). Later (III.6.191) the case of Dathan and his associates is cited as an example of how important, *a fortiori,* are Christian priests. In fact (197) 'the priests often bring into reconciliation not rulers nor kings but God himself when he is angry with them'. And in his last book, he returns to the thought of the fearful nature of the priest's function (VI.4.519, 520):

> When he invokes the Holy Spirit and consummates (*epiteleo,* a mystery religion word) the most terrifying sacrifice, and regularly handles the universal Master of all, where, tell me, are you to rank him? . . . Then even angels stand beside the priest and the whole sacred court of heavenly Powers, and the place round the altar is filled in honour of him (i.e. Christ) who is lying there.

The thought of the priesthood of all believers has completely disappeared before the priesthood of the clergy, with the exclusive capacity to control access to God. Though John Chrysostom in this work mentions other aspects of a priest's work, such as preaching and pastoral care, he defines him virtually in terms of the cult; he sees him as a Christian version of the Old Testament sacrificing cultic official, adorned with some traits taken from the hierophant of the mystery religions.

Very much the same sort of doctrine and atmosphere is to be found in Cyril of Jerusalem's *Mystagogical Catecheses.* This is the period when clerical celibacy begins to be enforced, when infrequent communion becomes a regular habit among the laity, when the sanctuary begins to be veiled with incense smoke and the clergy withdraw into it, when prayers begin to be said secretly, when the small but significant beginnings of the screen between laity and clergy are laid. Of this screen, at the stage when it had become a tall and solid *iconostasis*, A. H. Couratin has written ('The Eucharist before the Middle Ages', page 183):

> The Eucharist is a terrifying mystery; it is best performed, and indeed received, by the professional clergy; its prayers should be recited silently; its ceremonies should be carried out invisibly; only at certain great moments should it be displayed to the laity. The splendid screen is central to the majestic drama which is played out before and behind it.

In short, by the end of the 4th century the doctrine of Christian priesthood has developed to the point when the clergy are fast becoming a sacerdotal caste.

3

THE DEVELOPMENT OF EPISCOPACY
AND PRIESTHOOD

The Early Bishop

From this point onwards it will be necessary to follow the development of the concept of Christian priesthood in less detail than hitherto. The manner by which a doctrine of priesthood was attached to the existing ministry of the church and became an established and prominent feature of it has been traced. The outlines of the subject must now become broader and the pace of historical movement faster.

The reader must be reminded that the origins of episcopacy were not in any sense specifically sacerdotal. It is not true to say that episcopacy was instituted by Christ and his apostles. Monarchical episcopacy, of the kind in which the bishop is distinguished from the presbyter and the ranks above him, can only be found emerging in the 2nd century and was only accepted universally in the second half of it. It is not even accurate to say that originally bishop and presbyter were the same office and in consequence episcopacy developed out of presbyterianism. This has often been maintained, ever since Jerome at the end of the 4th century, perceiving that the historical pedigree of episcopacy as of apostolical institution was far from well established, claimed that there was no essential difference between a presbyter and a bishop. Jerome himself, of course, was a presbyter and (mercifully for the peace of the church) not a bishop. In a curious way both Presbyterians and Roman Catholics have used this argument, though they used it for very different purposes. In fact however it cannot be maintained that the bishop certainly developed from the presbyter. The church of Philippi, if we are to trust Philippians 1:1, had bishops and deacons but not presbyters, and the church of Jerusalem, if we are to trust the book of Acts, presbyters but no bishop. Acts, I Clement, the *Didache,* the Pastoral Epistles and Hermas witness that for some time and in many places at the end of the first and the beginning of the 2nd century bishops and presbyters were regarded as identical. But this does not force us to conclude that they always were identical in all parts of the church. It is very likely that originally some churches chose to institute presbyters and some to institute bishops—or at least functions undertaken by people whom they called *episkopoi*—and that in many places the two coalesced before the emergence of the monarchical bishop.

Unencumbered by an inherited theological pattern to which he might have felt he should conform, the bishop gradually became the chief officer of the church in virtually every respect. He was the arbiter of discipline, the leader in worship, the main administrator and distributor of the local church's wealth. By the beginning of the 2nd century at least presbyters and deacons and such lower orders of clergy as then existed were being subsidised by funds administered by the bishop; though he might employ deacons as financial assistants, he was ultimately responsible for finance. More important than this, the bishop was regarded as the repository of tradition and the man mainly responsible for knowing what Christianity is, teaching the faith and seeing that it was soundly handed on. He encountered some rivalry from the gifted teacher, from men of fame as Christian philosophers such as Justin, Pantaenus, Clement and Origen, but this rivalry was only occasional.

Apostolic succession in the 2nd and 3rd centuries did not mean succession by consecration, as it has meant in fairly recent years, as it has bedevilled the controversies of the 19th and 20th centuries; it meant the succession of sound and authoritative teachers of the faith in the office of bishops in the same place. When Irenaeus (*Adv. Haer.* IV.40.2) says that the bishop has 'a charisma of truth', he does not mean that the sacrament of holy orders confers on the bishop the power of discerning truth. That would be an altogether modern idea and one which even those who have the most exalted beliefs concerning sacraments would hesitate to embrace. He probably means that the church chooses and ordains as bishops those whom it perceives to have been endowed by the Holy Spirit with the charisma of seeing truth better, more clearly, more deeply, than others, what perhaps Paul would have called 'the word of wisdom'.

All these responsibilities combined to make the bishop pre-eminently a pastor, one who was responsible for the Christian formation of his flock. That is why when the concept of Christian priesthood emerged it attached primarily and significantly to the bishop rather than to the presbyter. These responsibilities also made the bishop a powerful figure, more powerful than any other official of the church. He was essentially the central figure in the church, the one through whose hands ran all the threads of control. He was not a ruthless power seeker. The 2nd and 3rd centuries did not see the church filled with ambitious prelates each seeking ever more control for the purpose of building up his private ecclesiastical empire. Apart from any other consideration, the extreme danger of being an important Christian official when the Roman government was always liable to attack the church in the persons of its leaders, would have discouraged such ambitions. Power flowed naturally and inevitably towards the bishop, and not always into willing hands.

Every office in the church was a development, and this was the way that circumstances caused the episcopal office to develop. The church used its officers for its own needs and purposes, and this monarchical bishop responded best to the needs and purposes of the early church. It is only necessary to read the letters of Ignatius of Antioch to see how anxious Ignatius is to support and foster the institution of monarchical episcopacy even though it is clear that the institution is a new one in his day and one for which he claims no apostolic foundation. The reader can see that he is convinced that it is the bishop alone who can rescue the struggling churches to whom he addresses his letters from foundering in the confused sea of sects and opinions and religions in the society in which they live, and can enable them to avoid the equally dangerous threat of collapse from internal strife.

The Bishop in the Middle Ages

Perhaps the most significant development during the Middle Ages as far as the doctrine of the priesthood was concerned was the gulf which was placed, at any rate in the west, between the presbyter and the bishop. During the period of the pre-Nicene church the presbyters were always closely associated with the bishop. They were his council, his staff; it was from their number that a new bishop was generally chosen. They received their authority, as they received their subsistence, from him. In as far as the bishop of this period was bound to keep in close contact with and to consult his council of presbyters, and had also to take account of opinion among the laymen of his see, it might almost be said that the bishop of the early church was a constitutional bishop, though not according to a strictly legal interpretation. Hippolytus' *Apostolic Tradition* in one place (39) gives the impression that the bishop met with his presbyters every morning. Certainly if they were called priests in the 3rd century it was because they were associated with the bishop and were thought to derive their priesthood from him. It must be remembered that the see or diocese until at earliest the beginning of the 4th century was a small affair. The bishop's seat or see church was usually situated in a town or city. Country bishops were rare or unknown. The bishop's jurisdiction would extend over the Christians in the town and those who lived at an undefined distance near the town. Parishes such as we know today were non-existent, and the very rudimentary beginnings of them appear only towards the end of the fourth century. Presbyters or deacons in a large town or a city might be in charge of a district in the town, as Felicissimus was associated with the Byrsa in Carthage and Arius with the district of Baucalis in Alexandria; but they were still thought of as the bishop's men, his staff, and not as clergy responsible for their own congregations and almost independent of the bishop.

During the 4th century a number of things occurred which began the process of divorcing the bishop from his presbyters. He often found himself saddled with legal or judicial duties as an arbiter to whom anybody, Christian or pagan, could appeal in order to hear and decide cases in civil (not criminal) law. His church would often find itself inheriting wealth from the gifts and legacies of the faithful. By the middle of the 4th century the Roman church was wealthy enough to excite the envy of many. In those days wealth very largely consisted in owning land. The bishop would have to administer the estates which his see owned. He would be responsible for the lives of the *coloni* (agricultural workers tied to the land) and slaves who worked on these estates and who were transferred to the church's ownership when the estates were transferred to the church. The Emperor Constantine began the practice of giving estates to the church when he gave to the bishop of Rome the handsome property which had been possessed in the past by the family of the Laterani but which was now owned by one of Constantine's own family; and St. John Lateran is still the Cathedral of the see of Rome. Further, the practice of holding church councils at central places in the Empire either of the whole church or for a large part of it, at which each bishop who could attend would represent his local church, must have interrupted the pastoral work of many a bishop and caused him to experience inconvenient absences from his see. Further, the innovation first introduced after the Council of Nicaea in 325 and perpetuated freely during the rest of the century, whereby the bishops of the losing party at important councils when a theological decision was taken were banished to parts of the Empire remote from the area of their pastoral responsibility, cannot but have added to this tendency.

Again, with the church's recognition by the Roman government the role of the bishop began slowly to change so that instead of being merely the head of the local Christian community he became the representative of everybody in the area covered by his pastoral responsibility. He tended to become the champion and defender of those in the place who were under any disadvantage or faced by any threat. We can see from the correspondence of such people as Basil of Caesarea and Gregory of Nazianzus how much business this new status threw upon the shoulders of the bishop. They exercised the right, which was well recognized by that time, of interceding for people condemned to death by the government. They make requests for various towns or districts to be granted remission of taxes for special reasons. They try to pull strings

71

on behalf of their own or their friends' relations who are in uncongenial posts or want promotion in the imperial service. They keep an eye on the monks, the hospitals, the guesthouses and the orphanages in their dioceses. John Chrysostom lists the responsibility of the bishop as 'the championship of widows, the care of the virgins and the troublesome business of being a judge' (*De Sac.* III.16.295).

By the end of the 4th century the Christian bishop was often one who walked with the great, who necessarily was involved in politics, especially if the secular authorities by altering divisions between the existing provinces threatened to either diminish or add to his territorial responsibility, and who had to know how to address correctly and tactfully all the different officials in the different grades of the imperial service, both military and civilian. All this necessarily tended to separate him from his presbyters. There were also always a number of bishops such as Hosius of Cordova in the early part of the 4th century, and Ursacius and Valens in the middle, and Gregory of Nyssa at the end of it, who were used as ecclesiastical diplomats and couriers by the Emperor himself and who must have spent a considerable part of their time away from their sees.

The 5th century saw the collapse of the western Roman Empire, and this long drawn out process, lasting from 407 when a vast horde of barbarians broke into the German and Gallic provinces from across the Rhine, most of whom never returned but settled within the bounds of the Empire, until 476 when, with every province of the former western Empire except the provinces of Britain occupied by a barbarian army and war lord, the last puppet Emperor was pushed off his throne in Rome, had necessarily a marked effect on the position of the bishop. The collapse of the Empire meant the collapse of the judicial system, the system of communications, the system of education, the legal system, and above all the administrative system all of which the Empire had maintained. It entailed invasion, disruption, confusion, often shortages and positive famine. It produced hordes of refugees, sporadic temporary risings by exasperated peasants, the collapse of trade, the extinction of culture, the decline of urban life. It meant the disappearance of many officials, some of

72

whom may have been oppressive or parasitic bureaucrats but some of whom were indispensable and capable administrators. It resulted in the permanent arrival on the scene of powerful but uneducated and (as Sidonius Apollinaris more than once remarks with disgust) unwashed barbarians who knew no Latin; it entailed an important shift in the ownership of property, and especially of land, towards the barbarian newcomers.

In these circumstances the local bishops very often became even more important figures than before. The bishop did not melt away before the barbarians, as the Roman officials did, but stayed where he was. He was very likely to be well educated, to have some experience in administration, to know how to handle finance. He would probably be a rich man. Everybody would respect him. When Sidonius Apollinaris at some point between 470 and 480 is commending in a sermon to the people of a Gallic town the man whom he has just chosen and ordained to be their bishop, he says in the man's praise that he has had experience enough to deal with both the togaed and the skin-clad type of men, i.e. both the Roman or Roman-trained official and the barbarian conqueror.

Consequently the bishop in the western world became more than ever identified with his local area, was regarded more than ever as the political and social leader of the people among whom his pastoral work lay. We find bishops all over the Empire called upon to deal with unprecedented situations and rising to the occasion. Synesius of Cyrene in the early years of the 5th century (410–14) has to organize resistance to invading barbarians from the south, and does so successfully. Germanus, who was bishop of Auxerre from 418 to 448, twice went to the imperial court to intercede on behalf of the people of Armorica, with whom he had some special connection, and at one point persuaded a Gothic king not to invade the territory of his see. Leo of Rome successfully averted the advance of the Huns on Rome in 452, and negotiated with the Vandals to obtain their evacuation of Rome after they had sacked it in 455, and in the year 451 Ammianus inspired the people of Orleans, his see city, to resist the Huns as they were besieging it, as Eunomius bishop of Theodosiopolis in the Eastern frontier of the Empire had led resistance to the besieging Persians

73

earlier, in 405. Salvian tells us that the Goths used Christian bishops as intermediaries with the Romans. Epiphanius bishop of Ticinum/Pavia negotiated treaties with Euric the Gothic king, Sidonius Apollinaris tried valiantly to preserve the territory of his see, Augustonemetum, from invasion, and as a result had to spend two years in exile at the hands of Euric. Patiens of Lugdunum in the middle of the 5th century spent much of the revenues of his see and of his personal wealth in importing corn at a time of famine caused by the invasions to succour the people of his see and of a wider area than that.

The aged Catholic bishop of Carthage, Deogratias, when the Vandal fleet and army returned from the sack of Rome with a large number of captives who were quartered indiscriminately in churches and large buildings throughout Carthage, spent his last efforts in bringing them help and comfort and finally died as a result of his labours. Epiphanius of Pavia was famous for his care for the helpless. Patrick tells us that in the middle of the century it was the regular custom of the church to ransom prisoners from the Franks by the instrumentality of clergy. Sidonius himself as bishop of Augustonemetum showed himself generous towards the helpless and needy. In one of his uninspired but revealing poems he gives a brief summary of the bishop's duties which may be compared with that given by John Chrysostom (see above, page 72): they are, to champion the lesser people, to care for the sick, strangers and prisoners, to see that the dead are decently buried, and to preach to the people.

Certainly the 5th century bishop in the west had a strenuous time, and we cannot criticize him for rising to the occasion when the crisis came. But this kind of activity, useful and suitable to his office though it was, inevitably tended on the one hand to distance him from his presbyters who, though they often must have acted as his staff, could not approach his authority and status, and on the other to restrict his purely pastoral activity, and to give him the air more of a public man than of a shepherd of souls. These activities and responsibilities must also have overshadowed the bishop's role as a cultic sacrificing priest, as they did not overshadow the role of the presbyter in this respect.

When the barbarian kingdoms of the west found their feet,

74

so to speak, when the confusion caused by repeated invasions, attempts on the part of the central Roman government to recover the lost territories, the movements of armies and insurrections of local populations had died down, and it became evident to everybody that the western Roman Empire was lost for ever and the barbarian kingdoms were permanent, then the role of the bishop became more important than ever. The barbarian kings encountered a serious lack of educated officials trained in administration. Christian bishops were both well educated and experienced in administering their dioceses. The successor kingdoms needed a legal system; in fact, they took over much of the taxation and administrative system of the former Roman Empire, but they needed men with legal knowledge to run it. Often they maintained for a long period two separate systems of law (as Theodoric did in Italy), applying to two separate sets of people living indiscriminately mingled among each other, the Romans and the barbarians. Bishops were people likely from their training and education to know something about law. Indeed after the middle of the 5th century, if we are to trust H. Marrou and P. Riché, there did not exist any uniform or widespread system of education in western Europe outside the church, which was bound to attend to education in order to train its clergy. It is not therefore surprising that once the successor kingdoms had been converted from Arianism (or, in the case of the Franks, paganism) to Catholicism, the barbarian kings began using bishops extensively as civil servants, in financial and legal administration. They were obvious and useful candidates for such posts.

During the early centuries of the successor kingdoms also, many sees became very wealthy. A glance at a history of the Visigothic Kingdom in Spain, for instance, will show with what determination many bishops pushed the fortunes of their sees and seized every opportunity to enrich the church, not collectively but especially in the form of their particular interests. In the Middle Ages (as to a large extent during the period of the Roman Empire) wealth took the form of land. A bishop on entering upon his see would automatically in many cases become an important landed proprietor. When Gregory the Great became bishop of Rome in 590 he inherited not only all

75

the lustre of the Roman see but also a huge extent of property in Sicily as well as in Italy. He immediately became by far the largest landowner in Italy. One result of this was the tendency of powerful families to capture sees for their own inheritance, much as powerful families annexed abbacies for themselves and made them hereditary in early medieval Ireland. When Gregory became bishop of Tours in 573, all the bishops of Tours except five had come from his family since the death of Martin of Tours in 397. Indeed the two centuries before the Carolingian Reformation at the end of the 8th and the beginning of the 9th centuries saw a serious corruption by the temptations of wealth and power affecting many bishops in France and Burgundy at least. The presbyters, who were now being transformed into parish priests as the parochial system began to form and to develop, were less exposed to such temptations.

By now too the institution of *Eigenkirche* whereby local landowners would build and endow a church, gaining the right of appointing the priest and of enjoying a share in the income deriving from it, had begun to appear. It is easy to see how strongly such a system as this would operate to drive a wedge between the remote bishop occupied with his secular cares and the local priest, restricted to his church in the country. In Germany, England and north-west Europe generally the manner in which the heathen tribes and nations had been converted, by the efforts of such missionaries as St. Willibrord, St. Boniface and St. Anskar meant that the newly founded dioceses tended to be territorially huge and the parochial clergy in consequence scattered and isolated. Here was another force which placed a distance between the bishop and the presbyter/priest.

When in the course of the Middle Ages the feudal system developed, the bishop met a new and complicating situation which separated him disastrously not only from his presbyters but also from his duty as a shepherd of souls, and even from his position as a champion of the local community and especially the weak and underprivileged among it. The key to the feudal system was the possession of land. Many sees possessed very large amounts of property in land. The local sovereign, be he king or duke or count, in theory owned the land and gave it to his vassals to enjoy on certain conditions; they were, for instance, bound to supply a certain number of soldiers to their suzerain on those occasions when he could legally call upon them, and if possible lead them into battle themselves. These duties applied and this station fell to the lot of the feudal baron.

Most bishops were feudal barons by virtue of the property attached to their sees, and they had to meet the demands of their position. A very few bishops were sovereigns in their own right in this system; the bishop of Durham, as head of a County Palatine approached this position in England but did not actually attain it. But the consequence of the bishops being involved in the feudal system in this way was that the duty of behaving like a feudal baron tended to override all other duties such as that of being a shepherd of souls, a champion of the poor or a sacrificing priest. The Bayeux tapestry shows Odo, bishop of Bayeux, fighting fully armed at the Battle of Hastings with as much relish as when he later assisted at the coronation of William I in Westminster Abbey, clad in such canonicals as were conventional then. Anna Comnena, the daughter of the man who was Byzantine Emperor when the armies of the first crusade reached Constantinople at the very end of the 11th century, was shocked and disgusted to discover that among the western barbarians bishops actually led armies and fought in wars, and records her horror in her history. Along with the duty of maintaining soldiers the bishop involved in the feudal system would usually find himself in charge of a court of law; here he was no longer the innocuous arbitrator in civil suits, as the 4th century bishop had been, but a judge with full powers in both civil and criminal cases, powers which included the right to imprison and to put to death. It was not until the beginning of the 19th century that the Archbishop of Dublin lost the last vestiges of his right to rule his liberty in Dublin, and that the prison belonging to the bishop of Durham was finally pulled down.

From the 12th century onwards, when the pattern of national kingdoms distinguished by language and to some degree culture began to emerge, the medieval king began to use the medieval bishop not merely as one of his barons but as a regular resource for supplying the administrators of his kingdom. He also, conversely, began to find bishoprics very useful as a means of rewarding his officials in the higher civil service. The holders of the major sees in England, for instance, Canterbury, York, Winchester and Lincoln, would become statesmen as well as ecclesiatics by virtue of holding their sees. Most of the great offices of state were filled by bishops during the period of the Plantagenet kings. The popular image of the bishop therefore became inevitably one of a ruler, a judge, a man involved in high politics, a warrior or a statesman or a financier rather than that of a priest or a shepherd. At a rather later period Cardinal Beaufort, who was bishop of Winchester during the first half of the 15th century, was able in 1427–29 to equip and to lead his own army against the Bohemian Hussites, as well as playing a leading part in the politics of his day during the whole of his career. He started with the advantage of being a member of the royal family. But an able commoner who was exalted to a leading see could have disposed of not much less power than Beaufort if he played his cards carefully.

The result of the bishop in the Middle Ages becoming a landowner, a baron, a judge, a ruler and a statesman was that inexorably his role as a shepherd of souls, as a leader of the local Christian community, was lost. There were medieval bishops who strove, not without success, to remember and enact their pastoral role, such as Hugh of Lincoln and Grosseteste of Lincoln and Richard of Chichester, but they were swimming against a strong tide and they must have formed the exception rather than the rule. Others frankly accepted the situation and enjoyed it. T. M. Parker (*Apostolic Ministry*, page 385) quotes the 11th century Archbishop of Rheims, Manasses, as saying, 'What a fine thing it would be to be Archbishop of Rheims if one did not have to sing the mass!' It will be recalled that Talleyrand complained of the same tiresome obligation when he was bishop of Autun just before the outbreak of the French Revolution. But these anecdotes serve to remind us that bishops, however much they were distracted from their pastoral duties, continued to be regarded as priests and, inasmuch as they had to celebrate mass, to function as priests. Their role as cultic sacrificing officials was not forgotten, even when their role as pastors had been wholly buried under other pressing and exacting responsibilities.

And yet their status as priests certainly suffered from this

78

medieval transformation. The priest *par excellence* during the period of the ancient church had been the bishop, and the presbyter was only a secondary priest. But during the Middle Ages the emphasis shifted. The presbyter became the representative example of priesthood rather than the bishop. It is the word presbyter which is corrupted into a word for priest in most of the vernaculars which arose out of Vulgar Latin during the Middle Ages, not *episcopus* (Italian *Prete*, French *Prêtre*) and which appears in German *Priester*, Swedish *präst* and English *priest* (but note Spanish *sacerdote* and Irish *saggart*). While the bishop was occupied in his administrative, judicial, political or even military duties, the presbyter was for the most part carrying on the presbyteral duties in his own parish, providing a continuity and a stability which the bishop could not supply. And in the conditions which prevailed during the Middle Ages the most obvious, most regular and most important presbyteral duty was that of celebrating the mass. This was the place where everybody met him and saw him. He was not prominent as a teacher, because he was often not educated enough to teach. Nor—in spite of the survival of a large number of sermons from the period of the Middle Ages—can he have been an effective and successful preacher, in most places and at most times; he was not well enough educated for that either. His pastoral duties outside the church building itself were reduced to a stereotyped list of activities which could become almost purely mechanical. But he could and did regularly and officially celebrate the mass in much the same place at much the same time. The presbyter therefore became the priest in a much more central and significant way than the bishop was. It was he who controlled the sacraments. It was he who stood for God in the sight of most men.

His priesthood was of course defined almost wholly in terms of the eucharistic cult. And as eucharistic doctrine developed so the doctrine of the priesthood and the doctrine of holy orders developed. The doctrine of how precisely a change takes place in the bread and the wine when they are consecrated in the eucharistic rite became more and more definite and carefully formulated, culminating in the articulation of the concept of transubstantiation by the Lateran Council of 1215. Correspondingly, the doctrine of what is conferred by priest's orders developed, and the doctrine of what exactly is the essential part in the making of a priest. It was determined that the priest, once ordained, possessed, not merely authority to consecrate the bread and the wine so that they became the body and blood of Christ, but also the power (*potestas*) of consecrating them so as to effect this conversion.

In popular thought and piety, if not in formal theological definition, all sorts of ideas were entertained concerning the power of the priest. He could call God down from heaven and confine him into a piece of bread. Further, he could (as development of religious thought in the later Middle Ages turned in this direction) offer Christ's sacrifice on behalf of the living and—perhaps more important—on behalf of the dead. He could control the eternal welfare of souls in purgatory as he said (or did not say) masses for them. The priests became the key figure in the vast system of post-mortem activity which covered Europe with chantry chapels and sustained thousands of mass-sayers who existed for this supernatural transaction alone.

When Pope Eugenius IV was asked to define the essential 'matter' of the sacrament of orders in 1439, i.e. what part of the rite was indispensable, it was natural that he should declare that it was the *porrectio instrumentorum*, the giving to the candidates for orders the symbol expressing the meaning of their order, in the case of priests the paten with the bread and the chalice. He was only confirming what the scholastic theologians had already conjectured. Another development of the doctrine of priesthood was that priest's orders conferred an indelible character, that is an ineffacable quality given to the soul, as much as did, for instance, baptism or confirmation, though of course of a different sort, so that once a man was a priest he must of necessity always be a priest, do he what he may, whether he liked it or not, apart from what sort of life he led or what activities he indulged in.

Conversely, the theology of episcopacy, in contrast to the functions of the bishop, became depressed as that of the priest was enlarged. In the late Middle Ages it was widely held that the bishop was no more than a particularly important priest, a priest endowed by the church with special powers, but ultimately no more than a priest. By this theory both bishop and priest were being defined by their cultic function, and further the priesthood of the bishop was being measured by the priesthood of the presbyter, and not vice versa, as was the case in the ancient church. The theology concerning both offices, of course, rested implicity on the assumption that Christ had, in the persons of the apostles, directly instituted priestly officials in the church, and that the medieval hierarchy derived its authority by its own line of succession through consecration directly from Christ independently of the rest of the church. That the bishop at the end of the Middle Ages found himself reduced, so to speak, theologically while he was exalted socially and politically, he owed not only to the fact that he had been forced into a largely non-theological, non-spiritual role, but also to the enormous increase in the power of the Papacy and the development of theology about the power and status of the Pope which tended to some extent to overshadow all bishops who were not the bishop of Rome.

The Reformation and Counter-Reformation

The Reformation in the 16th century brought the whole concept of priesthood sharply into question. To the reformers, the late Medieval church seemed nothing more than a vast machine designed to exploit God. God's grace was mechanically channelled through the priesthood to those who used the sacraments irrespective of whether they had sincere penitence or sincere faith. The sacerdotal system was being exploited in order to gain for Christian people spurious merit in this world and illusory remission of punishment in the next. God was regarded as a Deity capable of being manipulated, restricted in sacraments and controlled by the mass-saying priest. The gratuitousness of grace and the sovereignty of the Word of God were alike mocked by this system. Above all the reformers objected to the medieval doctrine of eucharistic sacrifice and offering. It meant that men can achieve their own salvation by paying for masses; it was a reversion to the Jewish sacrificial cult; it placed a priesthood between man and God, in exclusive possession of the access to the means of grace, in such a way that man was prevented from approaching God in humble faith and trust, which is the only way of approach pleasing to God. It abolished the priesthood of all believers. Such were the objections to the late medieval doctrine of priesthood, and to all that flowed from it, which presented themselves most vividly to the reformers.

They struck at this doctrine of priesthood wherever they gained control of the local church. They attacked the doctrine of transubstantiation which gave the celebrating priest so unique and impressive a power. They brought the clergy out of their position as a sacerdotal caste by encouraging them to marry. They devised new liturgies and new forms of worship in which the mass was turned into a communion of the whole congregation, a thanksgiving service for redemption, and even a commemoration of Christ's atoning work and little more. They resolutely rejected any doctrine of sacrifice and offering except the offering of ourselves, our souls and bodies, and the sacrifice of a pure and contrite spirit and of prayer and praise. Many of the reformers abolished the office of bishop altogether and reduced the priest to a presbyter again. Many too in their determination to eschew the dreaded oblation doctrine abolished eucharistic vestments and many traditional eucharistic ceremonies. Some abandoned a fixed liturgy altogether.

With the traditional ministerial offices there necessarily disappeared the traditional doctrine of apostolic succession. The reformers found it relatively easy to agree on points of doctrine associated with what they regarded as the great scriptural truths, such as the sovereignty of grace and justification by faith and the supremacy of scripture over late tradition. On the subjects of the sacraments and ministry they differed because (though for the most part they did not realize this) on these two subjects the witness of scripture is uncertain and fragmentary. But they all agreed that the conventional, traditional, indeed in a sense the Catholic doctrine of priesthood and all that went with it must be rejected, as contrary to the plain meaning of scripture.

The Roman Catholic Church, once it had recovered from the first shock of the Reformation and was launched upon the Counter-Reformation, embraced more warmly, so to speak, the medieval doctrine of priesthood and its corollaries. Tran-

82

substantiation, the priesthood as the sole guardians of access to the means of grace, the sacerdotal system of the ministry, the task of the priest to offer sacrifices on behalf of the living and the dead, the doctrine of apostolic succession which traced priestly authority in a line of hierarchical succession independent of the rest of the church, the submerging of the concept of the priesthood of all believers, the definition of priesthood in terms of the cult—all these the church of the Counter-Reformation emphasized with a more developed precision and a severer rigour even than before. The shock of the Reformation caused the Roman Catholic Church to codify and tidy up its doctrine rather than to reform it. Its doctrine became polemical, eristic, apologetic, embattled; and in the middle of its battle array was placed the conventional, traditional doctrine of the priesthood. Even the tendency to play down the priestly status of the bishop, and to regard him as far as his sacerdotal status went as only a magnified priest, was perpetuated in the church of the Counter-Reformation.

The Anglican Bishop

It would not be possible, even if it were within my competence, to trace the doctrine of ministry finally achieved in each of the Reformation traditions. Some were conservative, like the Scandinavian Lutherans. Some were very radical, like the Anabaptists. None left the traditional office and doctrine of priesthood untouched. We shall confine ourselves here to examining the fate of priesthood in the Anglican tradition.

The manner of treating this ancient tradition in the English Reformation was peculiar, if not actually unique. The office of bishop and of priest were retained unimpaired. Bishops continued to be consecrated and priests ordained in an uninterrupted series or succession. What was called the apostolic succession was preserved unbroken. Even if one were to entertain doubts about the validity in this respect of the consecration of Archbishop Parker (and it is now generally reckoned by scholars of all traditions that no serious doubts can be entertained on this subject), the full succession of canonically valid orders conferred by bishops who had been consecrated by the old ordination rites was preserved, owing to a peculiar combination of circumstances, in almost all the Irish sees, and bishops consecrated in this succession later took part in enough English consecrations to render any lingering doubt about the vadility of English ordinations unnecessary.

But the Anglican reformers deliberately and explicitly gave a new meaning and interpretation to these two offices of bishop and of priest. The old concept of a sacerdotal priesthood was rejected. To be more precise, exactly what was rejected was the practice of defining a priest in terms of a sacrificial cult, indeed in terms of any cult at all. He was described in the ordination service and in the Book of Common Prayer in a number of new and suggestive ways, as a watchman, a steward, a shepherd. His pastoral responsibility towards his people, and his responsibility to teach sound doctrine were emphasized; and at the moment of laying on of hands the following words were said:

> Receive the Holy Ghost for the office and work of a priest in the Church of God, now committed unto thee by the imposition of our hands. Whose sins thou dost forgive, they are forgiven; and whose sins thou dost retain, they are retained. And be thou a faithful dispenser of the Word of God and of his holy sacraments, in the name of the Father and of the Son and of the Holy Ghost. Amen.

It looks very much as if the Anglican Church had reverted, not to the Pauline, but to the pre-Cyprianic church in its doctrine of priesthood. There is no mention here of offering sacrifices on behalf of the quick and the dead, no *porrectio instrumentorum* (or rather the Bible has been in this ceremony substituted for the paten and chalice). There can be no doubt at all here of the church's intention to ordain a priest; the order is called that of priest and not simply of presbyter. But it is a priest carefully defined in other terms than those of a sacrificial cult. Of course he is empowered to celebrate the eucharist. But he is not defined by this power.

In the consecrating of a bishop nothing whatever is said in the consecration service of the Book of Common Prayer concerning his priesthood, even though it is well understood that as a bishop he will ordain priests and that he is already a

84

priest himself. It looks very much as if we have here a curious Anglican vestigial form of the medieval doctrine, that, as far as priesthood goes, the bishop is only a priest with some additional powers. But there is no doubt left in this service that it is a bishop which the church intends to make. And his office is defined in terms of his pastoral and teaching and governing authority, with particular reference made to his responsibility for looking after 'poor and needy people and all strangers destitute of help'. This bishop is to be found neither in Cyprian nor in Hippolytus but (if we are to look for him anywhere in antiquity) in Irenaeus. In the case of the ordination of all three orders, bishop, priest and deacon, the Book of Common Prayer makes the assumption, conventional until the 16th century but a matter of debate and controversy from then on, that all three orders were instituted by Christ or his apostles.

Such was the Anglican Reformation as far as it touched the priesthood: in some respects the product of its age; by no means altogether consistent nor carefully worked out; but clear enough in its main intentions and structure. Obviously the intention was to maintain the traditional, age-old offices of bishop and of priest, but to rid them of any possibility of being defined in terms of the eucharistic cult. Its intentions were courageous and admirable. It was perhaps one of the more successful examples of a genuine reformation of the church by the standard of scripture. And it resulted in a ministry which was full of fruitful possibilities for the future.

But these possibilities remained for several centuries largely unrealized, and the reason for this was that the medieval conception of the bishop's status and functions continued for centuries to linger on, bedevilling the intentions of the reformers. The Anglican Reformation was accomplished very largely by the activity of the Crown; Henry VIII, Edward VI and Elizabeth in different ways were the main architects of the changes in the structure of the church, though Cranmer and Jewell and Hooker may have contributed the doctrine. Thus the intention of the consecration service for bishops was to revert to the bishop as a pastor and a teacher and an administrator of his diocese, but the Sovereign saw to it that he remained a state official. The Tudor state and later the Stuart state needed bishops as political officers, and it was as political officers that the crown continued to use the bishops of the Church of England, the Church of Wales and the Church of Ireland for two centuries after the Reformation.

They were votes in the House of Lords, propagandists for government policy in the country, rich and powerful figures in the politics and opinion-forming media of the country. They were capable of suppressing the Roman Catholics and keeping the Puritan extremists at bay. They were more likely than any other body of men to support the crown and its policies through thick and thin because they had been appointed by the crown and regarded themselves as the servants of the crown. When James I said, 'No bishop, no King,' and when Charles I insisted on forcing an episcopalian system on Scotland and Charles II suppressed civil liberties and provoked a civil war in that country on behalf of an episcopalian polity, they were not doing this because they were deeply impressed with the pastoral advantages of episcopacy or profoundly convinced of the invincible superiority of the apostolic succession, but because they regarded the bishop as a political animal, and one which was safely on their side.

When the Puritans in England or the Presbyterians in Scotland in the 16th and 17th centuries looked at the Anglican bishop, they did not see a devoted pastor spending his time spreading true religion and sound learning among his clergy. They saw a man appointed by a political agency, the crown, usually from political motives and for political ends, a man who was compelled to spend most of his year in London transacting the business of the crown, one who was equipped by the government to carry out the government's policy. The early reformers had appealed from the authority of the Pope to the authority of the godly prince, alleging highly debatable Old Testament precedents for their appeal. The Anglican Church went further than any other reformed tradition in realizing the results of this policy. It was conservative in retaining the office of bishop in apostolic succession. But it was very radical in permitting the bishop to be almost wholly controlled by the king. The Lutherans might profess that they welcomed the doctrine of the authority of the godly prince. But there were hundreds of Lutheran pastors, not all of whom might be of the same mind. There were only 25 English diocesan bishops. It was not difficult for the king, who had appointed them all, to make them do what he wanted.

The gulf between the bishop and the presbyter, between the diocesan and the parish priest, therefore, remained unbridged in the reformed Anglican tradition. The Anglican priest might represent a new form of priesthood, disencumbered of his sacerdotal ideology, but the Anglican bishop remained in most essentials the medieval bishop, unable to become what his consecration service said that he ought to be. As the 18th century went on, it is true, the Anglican bishop became less powerful, less of a state official, unless he was an Archbishop. But he was not less of a politician appointed on political grounds for political purposes, either for the sake of his vote or as a means of satisfying, reconciling or winning over some powerful person whom the Prime Minister (rather than the crown by now) wished to please. And he made no progress worth mentioning towards closing the gap between himself and his clergy. This was not simply because he did not want to; it was because he was prevented from doing so by his duties in London and by the enormous size of his diocese. Thomas Wilson created a legend for himself by his careful pastoral attention to his diocese during the 18th century. But he was bishop of the tiny diocese of Sodor and Man, with a very small territory to cover and almost no political influence to distract him. But most 18th century bishops could not travel round their dioceses; they could not become John Wesleys; Wesley had no seat in the House of Lords. The world was his parish, but he had no government pulling at his coat-tails.

It was not until the 19th century, when the bonds between church and state were loosening, when the Anglican bishop was rapidly losing his political power, when the government began to let bishops become what some of them at least wished to be, that the Anglican bishop was given an opportunity to behave in his diocese as he was urged to do when he was consecrated. Even then it was beyond the shores of England that the best and brightest examples of Anglican episcopacy operating properly can be found: in missionary dioceses; in the Church of Ireland freed by the blows of W. E. Gladstone's axe from the chains of establishment, in Canada and in the United States of America. In these places he was free to be an authentic

87

bishop to his clergy and to his people also. There the pastoral element in his office was able to overcome the political. There his diocese, though it might be large in area, contained a manageable number of parishes.

It is true that the Anglo-Catholic Movement in the Anglican Communion during the 19th and early 20th centuries produced examples in some places of a deliberate reversion to the medieval doctrines of priesthood, and of the eucharistic offering and sacrifice. But as the Movement never succeeded at any point in altering the Anglican Ordinal in order to include or express these interpretations of episcopacy or priesthood, it is not greatly significant for our argument, for what is important in this area of doctrine is not what the particular bishop or priest would like to be or would like to think he is, nor how he interprets the formula by which he is ordained, but what was the intention of the church in conferring holy orders upon him. And that has always been clear and has been unchanged ever since the Anglican Church reformed its Ordinal in the middle of the 16th century.

Such, then, is a survey of the institution and doctrine of Christian priesthood, as careful and detailed as the scope of this work will allow in tracing the beginnings and early development, but necessarily more sketchy and generalized in following the later history. The next chapter will attempt to consider the value and authority of this doctrine, and to estimate how (if at all) it can be understood and realized in the age in which we now live.

4

THE MEANING OF CHRISTIAN PRIESTHOOD

The Significance of the Ministry

As we try to assess the meaning of the historical development of Christian priesthood which has been traced in the pages of this book, we must establish quite clearly what is the account and the theology of ministry upon which the whole argument of the book rests. It assumes that any theory of ministry which states that official ministers of any name or form as we know them today in the church, and have known them for fifteen centuries and more, were instituted by Christ and his apostles is wrong, is based on a false premiss and cannot result in a satisfactory theory of ministry. The understandable but misleading desire to identify in the pages of the New Testament one's own form of ministry, to throw over it the glamour and authority of dominical or apostolic foundation, to trace its pedigree proudly back to the beginning, must be resisted. That will-o'-the-wisp, apostolic succession, in the traditional and conventional meaning of that term, over which so much ink has been spilt, for which such extensive claims have been made, must be abandoned. And, as there are no prizes in this investigation, that which has often been regarded as the alternative to apostolic succession, the scriptural ministry, the ministry which while claiming no institution from the apostles, is regarded as authorized in the New Testament, as a form behind which, without paying particular attention to its origins, the authority of the new Testament can be said to stand, a ministry which has been there since the time of the primitive church and is supported by its authority, must also be rejected. The evidence suggests that neither of these things existed in the time of Paul, and therefore that they did not exist in the time of the primitive church.

This is not to say that an apostolic ministry does not exist and that a ministry may not be either scriptural or non-scriptural, but it is maintained that it cannot be so in the senses outlined above. It is possible to argue that one or more particular forms of ministry express and realize the apostolic mission of the church and are therefore in that sense apostolic, reproducing the apostles' mission and activity. And, as we shall see later (pages 96–99) it is possible to judge some types of ministry to be non-scriptural in that they deny or restrict the life of the church and the proper advancement of the gospel as these are depicted for us in the scriptures.

The account of the relation of the church to the ministry given here argues that the body which possessed authority in the beginning was the whole church, which can be authentically represented in its local manifestations, and that if people at any point and in any way exercise ministry they do so because this ministry has been given to them by the church, not because they or their predecessors were directly appointed by Christ or his apostles. In the earliest period authority and spontaneity, decision-making and freedom, charismatic calling and order, were combined without any of these elements excluding or infringing the operation of the others. All Christians regarded themselves as equally members of the body of Christ. All were united in a common bond of love and faith. All acknowledged the presence of the Holy Spirit who gave to different individuals different talents, capacities, callings and even characteristics (such as power to exhibit faith).

Authority itself rested in the church as a whole, which was a holy priesthood, a royal nation, an elect people. Instead of conceiving of Christ as handing authority over to, or rather as conferring authority on a ministry, official ordained ministers (whether Pope or bishops or priests or presbyters), we must think of him as conferring authority upon the church as an organic whole. I do not like the term 'handing authority over to', because this suggests that Christ was saying 'Occupy till I come', that he was making the church his substitute while he was absent. This is one reason for objecting to the description of the church as 'the extension of the incarnation'. The incarnation does not need extending. Christ has not left his church to

90

carry on during the tea-break of this present age. He is present in it in his Spirit, and its authority is his present authority. But that authority, given to and realized in and expressed by the church, is possessed by the whole church together, not merely by one part of it, called the ministry or hierarchy. No such ministry nor hierarchy existed in the beginning and therefore it cannot have been given authority by Christ in the flesh.

It may be objected that this conception of the church's authority is democratic or populist or even communist. Clearly there is some likeness to a democracy here, though not to western liberal democracies, for there was no head-counting in the primitive church nor taking decisions by majorities, and not to Marxist totalitarian democracies either, for there was nothing in the primitive church corresponding either to the party or to the proletariat as distinguished from the bourgeoisie. But the fact that we can see a democratic aspect in this account of the authority of the primitive church is not in itself sufficient to discredit such a theory of its authority. It is not only possible, it is likely, that our modern experience of democracy has enabled us to perceive this democratic nature of the church which was hidden from earlier ages which knew only oligarchies or monarchies or autocracies and were incapable of recognizing the nature of popular authority. They were quick enough to detect elements of constitutional monarchy or oligarchy there, but their historical experience was not sufficient to enable them to conceive of the type of organic, formless, popular authority which resided in the primitive church.

This authority came to every Christian at baptism. Then each was given liberty in Christ, union with Christ, life in the Spirit and an obligation to spread the message and to live out its meaning in his or her life. These are the elements which constitute the priesthood and election and responsibility, and so the authority, of the primitive Christian community, and it was these things which gave that community its expansive power, its capacity for reconciling apparent opposites, its self-confidence and its character and identity. This type of charismatic, initially eschatological, organic, authority which might in the last century have been called spiritual and in earlier centuries mystical, lies at the heart of the church's life

91

and must deeply affect our understanding of ministry, authority and priesthood. It rules out the possibility of the church deriving its authority from a ministry or hierarchy who have received their commission directly from Christ or his apostles or their successors independently from the rest of the church and have handed on this authority in a line of succession which retains this independence of and control over the rest of the church.

If an official ministry consisting of permanent officers occupying offices to which they succeed and to which they are appointed by formal ordination is to develop, it must be regarded as developing from the primitive church which originally did not possess such a form of ministry. And it must be thought of as a ministry representative of and appointed within and not independently of the rest of the church, bearing authority delegated by and expressive of the whole church, not as exercising a commission given by another authority than that of the church, to rule it or instruct it, as it were from on high or from outside. Such an expressive ministry has as its aim and authority to enable the church to become more truly the church (as has been expounded by A. T. Hanson in his book *The Pioneer Ministry*). Its business is not to oppress or restrict the church (though it may well be its task to govern the church), but to enable the church to realize itself, to become what it is, to move from being the empirical church to becoming the church in God's design.

The Official Ministry

As we know, an official ministry in the sense described above did emerge. By the middle of the 2nd century it was established everywhere in one form or another, and by the end of that century monarchical episcopacy, in which the bishop was distinguished from and raised above the presbyter and the deacon, was universally accepted. Was this a disaster, a hardening of the arteries of the nascent church, a stereotyping of its doctrine, a stifling of its life in legalism, moralism and institutions? It is easy to assume that this was so, that in the 2nd century the church lost its innocence, its spontaneous charis-

92

matic power and immediacy, which it was never able to recover until the 16th century, or perhaps the 20th. It is certainly true that with the official ministry appeared a concern for rules of conduct, a search for precedent, a harking back to a spurious apostolic authority, a failure of charismatic enthusiasm and prophecy and a tendency to regard Christianity as a series of doctrines rather than as an achievement of new being. That the first half of the 2nd century at least represents an *Abfall,* a trough rather than the crest of the wave in the voyage of the ark of the church, can scarcely be denied. Was the appearance of an official ministry just one more example of this falling off? Was it born out of weariness by disillusion?

This kind of argument is quite unrealistic. The church developed the official ministry because it needed the official ministry, neither in response to the demand of a logical significance attaching to the offices assumed, nor as a kind of hedge against disillusion and fading enthusiasm. In the history of a great many institutions and religions the first fine careless rapture is succeeded by a period of sober consolidation. The primitive church could not have continued indefinitely in its state of primordial charismatic bliss. Institutions and organisms grow and develop, and have to face the onset of time. The church was compelled to undergo what Charles Williams called 'the reconciliation with time'. The world was not, after all, going to come to an end almost immediately. The second coming of Christ never materialized. Pressures and problems both ouside the church and within it made it essential for the church to develop a permanent ministry, and if permanent then official and if official then ordained.

To say that the development of such a ministry meant a loss of power is absurd. There is absolutely no evidence that the church grew less rapidly and exercised less attraction when it had developed such a ministry than before this development. Ostracism and persecution, the break with Judaism, the necessity of recognising itself as a society living in history, with a past to be idealized and future to be planned for, all combined to impel the church towards this development. The authority of the church became less diffused, more channelled and concentrated. Parallel with the official ministry there were developing other features of the church's life necessitated by

93

'the reconciliation with time', a baptismal creed, the canon of the New Testament, the rule of faith of the church, a more ordered disciplinary system. We can recognize here an authentic and proper development. There is no reason to assume that this official ministry was not in accordance with scripture. The names of the officials (though scarcely the form of the ministry as it had developed by the year 200) are to be found in the New Testament. More important, there is no reason for thinking that the actual form of the official ministry itself hindered that which was to be ministered being imparted as it should be, the gospel, the communication of the new being, the opportunity of experiencing God in Christ. The form of the ministry must be judged by what is ministered. I do not see how it can be plausibly argued that the ministry of bishops, presbyters and deacons, as they appear in the pages of Ignatius, of Irenaeus and of Tertullian, hinders the good news or stifles the life of the church or dilutes the truth of the revelation entrusted to the church.

It would be most unwise to attempt to reverse the development which resulted in the appearance of an official ministry. We cannot put back the hand of the clock of history. We cannot return unreflectingly, unconsciously to a period of spontaneity and improvisation. Experience cannot be undone and unlearnt. Such an attempt would only result in an artificial primitiveness, a kind of ecclesiastical nudism, the atmosphere produced by adults when they try to behave like children. Attempts to do precisely this have of course often been made in the course of Christian history, especially by some groups among the radical Reformation in the 16th century, but it cannot be said that they met with much success. If by unanimous consent all Christian denominations were to abolish altogether tomorrow the distinction between clergy and laity, within ten years groups would begin appearing everywhere throughout the church who by their dedication, their expertise and their activity would earn the status, if not the name, of clergy. The Holy Spirit does not always call the church to stand still, and its moving onward may as well take the form of raising up official ministers as of inspiring prophets and visionaries.

An official ministry is part of tradition, and it is as inescapable as tradition. It is a device produced by the church in its journey through the world; perhaps it is the carapace with which it meets the pressure of history. As in the case of tradition it must be compared with and judged by the Bible, though, as in all cases of applying the norm of scripture, care must be taken as to how exactly this is done. But we can no more dispense with an official ministry than we can dispense with tradition. The dream of a wholly formless, wholly charismatic, wholly spontaneous church in the 20th century is a fantasy. The official ministry of the church is a permanent feature of its life. What we should ask concerning it is not, Should it be there?, but, What should it mean? How should it function? What is its relation to the church as a whole?

Sacerdotal Priesthood

Official ministry itself is a development. Within the tradition created by that development a Christian priesthood appeared. But we must here distinguish between two sorts of development. The official ministry was a quite new institution, having no continuity with the ministry of the Jewish religion, neither cultic sacrificing priest nor rabbi, carrying with it no theological significance, appealing to no tradition and no type, simply a development to meet the need of the church, taking such names as seemed suitable to express the very general functions of the various ministers. Priesthood was the application to this emergent ministry of a title which carried heavy significance, which had not one history but two, both of which contributed in some way to the part which it played and the meanings which were attached to it in Christian history, Jewish priesthood and pagan priesthood. No Christian priest emerged beside the bishop and the presbyter. What happened was that these two officials were called priests. Further, priesthood from the beginning corresponded to one important activity of Christ, whereas this could not be said as simply for episcopacy or for the presbyterate. There is one reference (1 Peter 2:25) to Christ being 'the bishop of your souls' in the New Testament, and one to his being 'a deacon of the circumcision' (Rom. 15:8), but nobody could seriously claim that bishops and deacons were instituted in order to correspond to such aspects of functions of Christ.

Priesthood, when it entered into Christian tradition, was a development, but a development of doctrine, of interpretation, rather than the development of a new institution. This doctrinal development had far-reaching effects upon the institutions of the church, upon the cult, the presbyterate and the episcopacy. But it was originally not the development of a new institution but the transformation in a new direction of existing institutions. What has to be decided here is, was the development of a Christian priesthood a right and proper, perhaps even an inevitable development, as, according to the argument of this book, the development of an official ministry was?

One immediate answer can confidently be given. What has been called sacerdotal priesthood certainly was not a right and proper development. By sacerdotal priesthood is meant the concept of priesthood which prevailed in the Middle Ages and which was rejected by all the reformed traditions in the 16th century but stoutly maintained as a fundamental doctrine by the Roman Catholic Church until at least the Second Vatican Council, and taught also in some form by the Orthodox Church. In this view the priest is defined by his cultic activity, his function in offering to God the sacrifice of Christ in the eucharistic rite. He alone has access to the means of grace, to sacraments, and exclusive control over them. He has the power of placing worshippers in the presence of God by his power to convert the elements of bread and wine in the eucharist into the body and blood of Christ, and this power is given to him in the sacrament of orders which gives him an 'indelible character' in his soul, so that he can exercise this supernatural capacity whenever and wherever he likes, even though he may owe obedience to rules and regulations which forbid him to do so indiscriminately and frivolously.

For instance, it is said that an insane French priest once went into a confectioner's shop, made the sign of the Cross and uttered the words *Hoc est corpus meum*. It became at least an open question whether he had not converted thereby every piece of bread in the shop into Christ's body; at any rate the Archbishop of Paris is said to have bought up and destroyed the contents of the shop. Or, to take an imaginary instance, if

96

during a diplomatic dinner at the Congress of Vienna, Talleyrand had toyed with a piece of bread supplied with the soup and made the appropriate gesture and said the appropriate words, would he not have produced the same supernatural effect in the bread?

Further, this concept of priesthood was deliberately modelled on, and consciously invoked as a precedent, the cultic sacrificing priesthood of the Old Testament, and relied upon the assumption that Christ himself had founded this priesthood and willed that it should be perpetuated in a line of succession or consecration independent of the rest of the church. Again this concept was essentially one of a sacrificing priesthood. Not only did the priest control access to salvation, but he, and he alone, could confer vitally important benefits and advantages in offering this sacrifice on behalf of the living and the dead, and it was thought in the later stages of the development of this doctrine of priesthood that some at least of those who had departed this life would hardly achieve salvation without such priestly assistance, assistance which was not of a general or undefined sort, but which was thought to be precisely, even mathematically, calculable. In this concept the priests constitute a sacerdotal caste governing the church by a commission which is separate from and not an expression of the commission given to the rest of the church. And finally, in the later stages of the history of this theory, at least in west, the distinction between the bishop and the priest, as far as sacerdotal powers is concerned, is unimportant. The bishop is measured by the priest, and is thought to be a kind of super-priest, a priest who has been given certain additional authority and additional faculties.

This concept of priesthood is not only unhistorical but highly undesirable. No priesthood was founded by Christ or by his apostles. No command was given to a sacerdotal caste to govern the church by some higher commission divorced from the authority of the rest of the church. The original officials upon whom the title of priest was conferred were bishops, not presbyters, and presbyters were thought to derive their priesthood from the bishop, reversing the relationship ascribed to them in later thought. The concept is not merely not to be found in the scriptures, where the word for a priest as

97

an official minister in the Christian church simply does not occur, it is actually un-scriptural, anti-scriptural. Not only the epistle to the Hebrews but also the whole thought of Paul, and many other passages in the New Testament too, make it quite clear that with Christ all sacrificing cultic priesthood, whether Jewish or pagan, has become insignificant and emptied of purpose.

Further, the confining of the means of grace to the priesthood is a flat contradiction to that liberty which the New Testament claims that Christ has brought to all who will accept it. All Christians are equally entitled to approach God in Christ freely and joyfully, in faith and love. The precious gift which Christ has brought, new being, state of justification, eschatological joy, entry into the kingdom of heaven, is the right and heritage of all. It is manifestly wrong for clergy or priests or any other official to claim, to teach, or even to boast that they and they alone can dispense this gift because they alone admit people to sacraments. In sacraments God offers himself to man, but man does not control him. Such an idea infringes the majesty, the transcendence, the freedom of God as well as restricting the freedom of Christians. Again, this sacerdotal concept of priesthood appears to obscure completely, if not actually to abolish, the doctrine of the priesthood of all believers. It drains believers' priesthood (or better the priesthood of all baptized people) all away into the priesthood of the clergy. It contributes to that tendency to create of the clergy a ruling caste controlling cult and sacraments, and sharpens the distinction between clergy and laity to the point where the clergy for most purposes are the church and the laity become at the best a dumb and docile flock acted upon rather than acting, and at the worst amateur voluntary Christians in contrast to the clergy who are paid professional Christians.

The more specifically eucharistic aspects of this sacerdotal concept of priesthood draw those who discuss them into very controversial areas of debate. Perhaps it is enough to say that the idea that priests (or anybody else) offer Christ as a sacrifice is highly debatable and not easy to reconcile with Paul's doctrine of justification by faith, and that the converting power of the priest's activity upon the bread and wine in the eucharist is also a most ambiguous doctrine which needs to be explored

98

with care and can only be accepted with many qualifications. And yet this last doctrine is in some ways the foundation stone of the sacerdotal concept of priesthood.

The great basic, incurable fault of this doctrine is, in my view, that it defines the priesthood in terms of the eucharistic cult. It makes the early Christian bishops and presbyters into sacrificing cultic priests, and subordinates all other aspects of their ministry to that. This was a serious and unjustified innovation, made in the western church in the 3rd and in the eastern church in the 4th centuries. It had important and far-reaching consequences for the ministry, for the church and for many aspects of Christian doctrine, almost all of which were disastrous and led ultimately more than any other purely theological contribution to the break-up of the western church in the 16th century. If Christians in the 20th century are to achieve a better understanding of scripture and of tradition and of Christianity as a whole, this sacerdotal concept of priesthood must be either discarded altogether or drastically modified.

True Priesthood

Is the concept of priesthood, then, to be discarded altogether, as many Reformation traditions have discarded it? I think not. However defaced and distorted in the history of Christian thought, and however fatally it has been attracted into the seductive possibility of becoming a cultic priesthood, the concept of priesthood is not itself either anti-scriptural or anti-Christian or necessarily incompatible with the great Christians truths. It has already been shown that a priesthood not defined in terms of the cult was ascribed to the bishop in the earliest stage of the history of Christian priesthood and that the Anglican communion ever since the Reformation in the 16th century has ordained priests who were not defined in cultic terms. Oliver Goldsmith in the year 1766—a period when nobody could accuse the Church of England of entertaining dangerously sacerdotal tendencies—says in the Advertisement to his *Vicar of Wakefield*, 'The hero of this piece unites in himself the three greatest characters upon earth; he is a priest, an husbandman, and the father of a family'. But the defence of a doctrine of Christian priesthood needs more than a quotation from Goldsmith to establish it. The following arguments may perhaps serve.

We should not overlook or scornfully reject the fact that a great many other religions besides Christianity, perhaps the majority of religions, have had priests. We have seen (see page 40 above) that the *Didascalia* makes a hesitant suggestion that pagan priesthoods are a pattern for Christianity. Of course Christianity did not take over the priesthoods of paganism wholesale. But it probably learnt from the example of pagan religions that most men find it difficult to understand or approach God without the aid of a man who in some sense stands for God, represents him, and feels called to devote himself to this representative ministry. If we at this late stage of the book ask ourselves how priesthood should be most generally defined, putting aside actual examples of Jewish or pagan or Christian priesthood, we should have to say that priesthood consists of a ministry of men or women who stand for God to their fellow-men and represent their fellow-men to God. This definition does not necessitate the person who exercises the priestly function having an exclusive monopoly of access to God, only that his function is to represent men to God and God to men. It is surely an impressive fact that a very large number of religions have had such persons; whether they were cultic priests or medicine men or any other sort of priests, this was, and was taken by their fellow-worshippers to be, their basic function. It suggests that there is something natural and universal about priesthood.

Next, it is significant that the early Christian concept of priesthood (as well as its later forms) insisted that the priesthood was a reflection and expression on earth of Christ's priesthood. This seems to me a valid conception, once we grant that it was right and natural and inevitable that an official ministry should appear at all. This official ministry was not unrelated to the priesthood of all Christians. It was inevitably in a certain measure a channelling and concentration of this priesthood, which was the church's priesthood and an expression and realization of Christ's priesthood. There is no reason why the existence of a number of official ministers called priests should thereby abolish or atrophy the priesthood of all

100

baptized Christians, provided that it is not held that these priests have exclusive access to or control over God's communication of himself in Jesus Christ, and as long as it is understood that they derive their authority as priests by delegation from the whole priestly body, and do not pretend that they have a special line of authority independent of this in a succession from Christ's institution.

Indeed, one can conceive of a priestly ministry on these terms which is in a powerful and impressive sense a reproduction of Christ's priesthood in that it is not a ministry that makes arrogant claims for itself and insists upon its privileges and powers, but gives itself unsparingly in Christ's service, reproducing his humility, his self-abandonment and his love. One can think not only of the real example of Fr. Damien and the fictitious one of G. K. Chesterton's Father Brown, but of the picture drawn by Keble in his poem, which must have many traits in it drawn from humble Anglican priests whom the poet knew:

> The Christian pastor, bowed to earth
> With thankless toil, and vile esteemed
> Travailing again in second birth
> With souls that will not be redeemed.

This is the picture of one who sees himself as commissioned to bring his people to God, who has orders, i.e. commands, to execute, a responsibility to God on behalf of his people, a word to preach, a discipline to maintain, a style of life and of piety to foster. But he is also one who must in many senses identify himself with his people, struggle for them, pray for them, think for them, plan for them, understand their problems and feelings and fears and hopes. There have been priests of all traditions who have emphasized too much that they stand for God to men, who have been tempted to tyrannize, to scold, to be hard and unfeeling.

There have been others in all traditions too who have erred in the other direction. They have so associated themselves with their people that they have forgotten God's calling in their anxiety to share men's condition, and have turned themselves into welfare officers or politicians or socialites or, at the worst, entertainers. Or they have allowed their sympathy

101

with the political enthusiasms, or even the selfish worldly interests of their flocks to blind them to the message which they should be delivering. Samuel Butler in *The Way of All Flesh* says that the flock of the Reverend Theophilus Pontifex would have been as much surprised to find anyone doubting Christianity as they would have been to find anyone expecting them to practise it. There are many ministers of religion, both Catholic and Protestant, at the moment in Northern Ireland who are afraid to speak to their flocks the honest word of reconciliation because such an utterance would deprive them of the sympathy, friendship and support of their people. But the Christian priest must combine concern for God with concern for man. He is essentially a go-between person, an *alter Christus*.

This kind of priesthood, not defined in cultic terms and therefore making no claims to exclusive power to give access to God, can coexist very well with other ways and means whereby other people can find God. The obligation for Christian worship and life to be in a sense communal, not individualistic, does not rest upon the fact that the clergy alone can put the laity in touch with God, and they therefore must gather together in church to be led by the priest, but on the communal, organic, collective nature of salvation whereby those who are redeemed are redeemed into a body, a company, a people. But though the Christian priest must not be defined by the cult, it is altogether fitting that he should be the main minister in conducting the cult. When he celebrates the eucharist the priest is acting for men to God and for God to men most representatively, most fully, most appropriately. The fact that his status is not defined by the cult need not lead him to undervalue either the cult itself or his part in it. He is, after all, as he celebrates, the concentration of the priesthood of Christ's people who leads them into their priesthood, not fulfilling it instead of them, as their substitute, but as their representative and spokesman and leader. And he has, by ordination, the authority of the church, the authority of Christ acting and ordaining in the church, not only to represent them to God but also to speak to them on God's behalf, in God's name. Even though he is not the only person to speak and act in God's name, still he bears that authority. The church has recognized

102

in him one who is fit to speak the word of wisdom and has ordained, commissioned him to do so, trusting in faith that God has done what at the ordination service the church prayed that he should do.

Corollaries of True Priesthood

Next, we must draw out certain consequences which arise from this doctrine of priesthood, a priesthood, which rests upon the priesthood of all baptised Christians, the priesthood of the church, and which relies upon no doctrine of apostolic succession and refuses to define itself in terms of the cult.

It must be made clear that it is the bishop who is the priest *par excellence*, not the presbyter/priest. Once the theory that priesthood was directly instituted in the church by Christ is abandoned, the idea that the presbyter is the original priest vanishes. The early church saw the bishop as the priest *par excellence* because it recognized him as the central and most significant minister in the church. Its instinct was, I believe, sound in this. It was only by default and by misadventure that the mantle of priesthood *par excellence* fell upon the shoulders of the presbyter. During the Middle Ages and for several centuries thereafter the bishop was distracted from his true function and character by being called upon to fulfil, or being tempted to fulfil, half a dozen roles which had no essential connection with his ministry—lawyer, civil servant, judge, financier, baron, governor, statesman, soldier. In particular the bishop of the *ecclesia Anglicana* was tied to the state with unusually strong bonds which did not seriously relax until long after the Reformation. This was a defacement and distortion of episcopacy. We cannot blame the leaders of those traditions who at the Reformation altogether rejected episcopacy for failing to see anything valuable in such examples of episcopacy as a Beaton or a Wolsey. During the Middle Ages the bishop grasped the secular power that was put into his hands; it was perhaps natural and inevitable that he should do so. But at the Reformation he paid dearly for the sweets of power. The reformers, their eyes fixed on the Bible, could not recognize the Christian shepherd in the remote official

103

disposing of great riches and power, the intimate associate of statesmen and often the tool of the government. We can see why in many instances they saw no purpose in retaining this particular ministry.

As we have seen, the Anglican Reformation ought logically to have reduced the role of the bishop to a more primitive and more acceptable pattern, that such a task was attempted, but that for several centuries the attempt was unsuccessful. The reformers in England retained the concept of priesthood for the presbyter, probably in this unreflectingly following the late medieval idea that the presbyter was and always had been the original and archetypal priest. They did insist that nobody could be a bishop who had not first been a priest; they allowed that the bishop was capable of conferring priest's orders on a priest, and therefore of course must be in some sense more of a priest than the presbyter. But it cannot be said that the Anglican reformers envisaged the bishop as the priest *par excellence*. We have seen that even if they had done so it is most unlikely that the state would have permitted the bishop to function in a way appropriate to this role. The state believed that it had more important things for the bishop to do. It was still dazzled by the dream of the medieval bishop, who ranked, as he did in chess, with the king, the queen, the knight and the castle, but who through the reigns of the Tudor and Stuart dynasty too often in fact performed the part of a pawn.

But in the 20th century it is time for the Anglican bishop to retrieve and vindicate his status and function as priest *par excellence*. Ever since the Anglo-Catholic movement during the second half of the 19th and first half of the 20th centuries there have been bishops standing in the tradition of that movement who have indeed vindicated such a priesthood for themselves; but unfortunately they have done so in terms of medieval sacerdotal priesthood, and as a result only made confusion about the meaning of priesthood in the Anglican tradition worse.

Now it is time for all Anglican bishops to realize that they are priests, but not priests in the sacerdotal sense. No Anglican bishop has any right to claim this. Pope Leo XIII was perfectly correct when in his Bull *Apostolicae Curae* (in 1897) he declared that precisely what was lacking in Anglican orders was the
104

intention to ordain priests who offer sacrifices on behalf of the living and the dead. His mistake was in imagining that this is and always has been the essential thing that makes a presbyter a presbyter or a priest a priest. His historical understanding was as defective as that of Eugenius IV when (in 1439) he placed this essential element in the *porrectio instrumentorum* (see above, page 80). Leo XIII had the credit of locating his historical error several centuries earlier than the period where Eugenius IV had located his; that is all.

What makes any minister a minister is the expressed intention of the church in ordaining him. This has always been the Anglican doctrine of intention, and it is a far more satisfactory one than the subjective and unverifiable Roman Catholic doctrine that this lies in the private intention of the individual person who ordains. The Anglican ordinal (which has not been seriously altered in any Anglican province since the 16th century) states quite clearly that it means to ordain a priest as a priest and a bishop as a bishop and adds a number of statements about the function and character of both. Quite justifiably it says nothing at all about offering sacrifices on behalf of the living and the dead. It is therefore quite inconsistent, illogical, and indeed absolutely untrue for any Anglican priest or bishop to say that he has been ordained as a sacerdotal priest in the sense described in this book. Private interpretations do not alter the effect of holy orders. It is therefore in a new sense, or rather in an old sense revived and reformed, that Anglican bishops ought now to begin thinking of themselves as priests *par excellence*.

I must stress that what I call for is that Anglican bishops should begin to think of themselves in this way, because I believe that many have for a long time been acting as priests *par excellence* in this way and have thereby acknowledged the justice of this doctrine. Very many Anglican bishops have for long acted as outstanding representatives of God to man and man to God and in proving themselves fathers in God to their clergy and their people have become excellent examples of a priestly ministry. And this judgement applies as much to bishops of the Church of Ireland, which can certainly be accused of no hankerings after a sacerdotal priesthood, as it has to any other provinces of the Anglican Communion. What is needed is a realization that, in performing this essentially pastoral role they are fulfilling a priesthood which should rightly be regarded as part of their office, and that if their priesthood is instead defined in cultic terms it loses rather than gains; it narrows itself and thereby distorts itself.

But it is not only a sacerdotal interpretation which can damage and deface this priesthood. If a bishop is given a diocese so large that he has to spend a disproportionate amount of time in administration, and in visiting the headquarters of his church in order to attend committees and synod meetings, leaving his priestly activities (as defined in the new sense of priesthood described in this book) to bishops without jurisdiction called suffragans or assistants, he is narrowing and defacing his priesthood too. This is a fate which has overtaken most of the bishops of the Church of England, whose dioceses are far too large for them to act in this priestly role in an adequate manner towards either their clergy or their laity. The size of their dioceses does not stem from considerations of administrative convenience but from the powerful vestigial influence of the Middle Ages in the Church of England. There were twenty five dioceses in England in the reign of Elizabeth I. Since then the population of England has multiplied at least six times. On this calculation there should now be at least one hundred and fifty dioceses. There are only fortyfour.

We next must ask whether the non-sacerdotal priest, as described here, enjoys a *character indelibilis* in the medieval sense, whether the reception of priest's orders imprints on his soul a quality which no circumstance can ever erase. The concept of a *character indelibilis* was originally applied to the sacrament of baptism and derived from the thought of Augustine on that subject. During the Middle Ages, when the scholastic theologians were occupied in making a systematic construction out of the various traditions and theologies which they had inherited from the past, they were anxious to systematize theology about the sacraments. They determined that the sacraments numbered seven, and that everything described as a sacrament must have a defined matter, a defined effect, and so on, and they attempted to apply this to every sacrament, even to so apparently indefinable ones as the so-called sacraments of penance and of marriage. It was in the
106

process of applying this type of reasoning to what they called the sacrament of orders that they decided that orders conferred a *character indelibilis*, as baptism and the rest did (though each sacrament conferred of course a different and appropriate *character*).

I do not think that anything at all is gained by indulging in this particular theological exercise. I believe that the scholastics were mistaken in attempting to produce a uniform and systematic theology applicable to all sacraments. What are called sacraments consist of a number of diverse ceremonies and practices which have grown up gradually during the history of the church only two of which, baptism and the eucharist, can certainly be traced to the institution of Christ or his apostles.

The scholastics, of course, could not know this. They thought that all seven sacraments were, in one way or another, of dominical or apostolic institution. But nothing is gained by treating these things as all amenable to the same theological treatment, and much lost in the resulting confusion. Confirmation is an excellent and useful rite. It is a wholesome and salutary practice for a Christian to confess his sins to a priest in order to ask for his counsel and advice and to seek the forgiveness of God for the quieting of his conscience. Marriage is an inestimable good, ultimately essential for the good of society as well as of the individuals concerned. But it is most unwise to treat these very diverse, highly heterogeneous practices and institutions as if they were all amenable to being called sacraments and brought under the same theological classification.

So it is with the so-called sacrament of holy orders. It is unnecessary and confusing to apply to it categories which may be useful for baptism but are here applied to a quite different activity of the church. If we refuse to group all sacraments under a single heading in this way, we are left with a situation in which we must simply say that we cannot generalize about the effect of holy orders upon the qualities of the souls of those who receive them, and to claim that we can is officious and misleading. That a priest should adopt a special and appropriate style of life and that this style should be intended to be lifelong and admit of no exceptions during holidays or at other times; that he should, in the words of the Book of Common

107

Prayer 'draw all his studies that way' and endeavour to form his life and the lives of his family in a manner in accordance with the gospel, is of course entirely true and by no means unimportant. But this is a quite different concept from that of the *character indelibilis*.

But if we deny a *character indelibilis* to a priest, do we allow him *potestas*, power conferred by orders and denied to those who do not receive orders? By power there is here of course not intended wordly or even spiritual influence, but a capacity to convert the bread and the wine in the eucharist into the body and blood of Christ, or into the sacrament of the body and blood, or even (to revert to earlier examples) into the antitype or symbol of the body and blood. It is tempting to agree that the priest, to whom the celebration of the eucharist is restricted, has some such power as this. Ascription to him of *potestas* of this sort sets him apart, gives him an advantage which others do not possess, and gives a solid meaning to the concept of priesthood. But the temptation must be resisted. To ascribe such a power to the priest is once again to define him by his cultic function, and this seems to me undesirable. Further, it tends to separate the action of the priest from the action of the church. The celebration of the eucharist then depends upon the presence and functioning of one man, not upon the gathered congregation calling upon God through Christ by the agency of this one man; on this view he would not represent the people of God, he would have power independent of his representative status.

Once again, such a doctrine depends upon a particular view of the theology of the eucharist which is not necessarily the only possible view. In fact the doctrine of priestly power sprang out of the eucharistic theology (or, to be more accurate, eucharistic piety) rather than vice versa. What the priest has is authority, authority to represent the church, whether in ordaining or confirming or in celebrating the eucharist. Faith can be satisfied with the authority conferred in the ordering of priests. In the eucharistic rite the church calls upon God in faith to bless the bread and the wine so that those who eat them shall receive the body and blood of Christ. Individual Christians who are present, worship and communicate, believe that God answers their prayers. But they must have confidence that the

108

person who in their name calls upon God to bless the elements is the authentic representative of the church, and not someone with no more authority than that of an individual Christian.

The church is not an aggregate of individuals, it is an organic whole, like one body with many limbs. Its representatives on such solemn occasions as these must therefore be organically representative; the church must make sure that they represent and are authorized by the whole church and are not acting under individual or partial or factional authority. This is the authority that the priest wields, and anyone who does not possess this authority should not presume to arrogate it to himself. If someone who does not possess this authority celebrates the eucharist, nobody can be sure that God will respond to the church's prayer and bless the elements. It is not that such a person lacks a capacity, a faculty, as a tone-deaf man lacks the capacity to distinguish a tune, or as somebody with no experience of motors lacks the capacity to drive a bus, or as someone who is not a dowser fails to divine water. It is that when the unauthorized person celebrates, faith has no ground to seize on, the Catholic Church is not authentically represented. What is lacking is not expertise or talent or faculty, but confidence.

In one other particular the priest obviously has an authority comparable to his authority in the eucharist, and that is in the power of the keys. The forgiveness of sins was something which the church, apparently from its earliest days, claimed to possess and exercised confidently. As far as we can make out from Paul's letters, he did not himself, apostle though he claimed to be, excommunicate or admit to communion. He recommended his churches to do one or the other. It was in the whole local church that the power lay, and, as has been indicated above (page 21) to quite a late date the whole local church exercised this privilege of judging penitents and sinners. As the emergence of an official ministry concentrated authority in the hands of the minister who represented the church, so the authority to forgive or retain sins, to communicate or excommunicate, was delegated to the priest. But, as in all other instances, he here represents the church. He does not derive this authority from any other source than from his standing in the church to represent it towards the individual

109

sinner or penitent. It is to the church, not to the ministry apart from and independently of the rest of the church, that Christ has given the power of the keys.

It is significant that when the concept of Christian priesthood first developed, it was not in cultic terms, but in terms of the power of the keys that contemporaries interpreted the title, as far as they interpreted it at all (see below, pages 39f). Further, at the Reformation the Anglican Communion specifically mentioned this power of forgiving or retaining sins at the most solemn moment of the ordination of a priest (see above, page 84). In the Church of England today the exercise of the power of the keys is, owing to historical reasons, rarely seen (though it is by no means simply in abeyance). But in the church overseas and in missionary areas it is a prominent and vital part of the church's life. It is indeed significant that almost all denominations (even in some places the Society of Friends) have found it necessary to exercise discipline in regard to admission to the eucharist on the mission field. Here the church has been forced to exercise its authority, and in the case of the Anglican Communion to do so through its priests. This is not to say that priests may not associate laymen with them in determining cases of discipline. It is very fitting that they should, not only for the practical good sense of such a procedure, but because this emphasizes the representative character of the priestly activity. This practice is in fact followed in several parts of the Anglican Communion. But the actual judgment should be given through a priest as representing the whole church.

It is perhaps unnecessary to add that in his preaching and teaching and pastoral work the priest represents the whole church. The fact that lay people nowadays also preach and teach and sometimes do pastoral work only means that the church has chosen to spread its authority more widely, more diffusely, in these respects. There is no reason why it should not do so when circumstances demand it, as they often do today.

It only remains to be said on this particular subject that a priest's calling and commission and authority is meant to be, and ought to be, life-long, permanent. He is required to shape his life in order to meet this commission from the church. This

110

life-long commission and commitment give a depth and weight and force to his authority which commissioning for a limited period could never give; what should mark him out from other men is not a life of celibacy (though he can choose such a life if he thinks fit), nor a segregation into a sacerdotal caste, but the seriousness and responsibility with which he undertakes the task which ordination has given him. This does not involve a *character indelibilis*, but it does demand a special life-style and a special dedication and if these are taken seriously they will imprint a recognizably priestly stamp (in the best sense of the word) on his character and behaviour, indeed on his whole personality.

Women as Priests

We must now face a difficult question, which is particularly clamorous today. Can women be ordained priests, and should women be ordained priests? The subject is usually debated as if it turned upon whether Christ himself did choose or could have chosen women as apostles and whether the apostles themselves ordained women. But this whole approach to the subject must be put out of court at once. As we have seen, Christ did not ordain anyone in our modern sense of the word ordain, and the apostles did not ordain anyone either. What Christ and his apostles might or might not have done by way of instituting female ministers is purely irrelevant, for they did not institute any ministers in our modern sense of the word.

It is indeed true that Christ did not choose any women to be apostles, that is, to be in the number of the twelve. That could be regarded as a point against the ordination of women. But on the other side we must notice, first that for a rabbi or popular teacher to choose feminine students or scholars would have been a startling innovation in 1st century Judaism with no precedents, certain to cause a scandal. Secondly, Jesus Christ certainly did associate with women to an extent which was unconventional in those days and even gave rise to talk. He spoke with the Syro-Phoenician woman (a gentile); he associated with prostitutes and socially outcast women and was able to make some of them into his followers. He had indeed a

111

regular following of women, some of whom (including his mother) formed the very first members of the infant church. Even more striking, if we are to trust the accounts of Matthew, Mark, Luke and John, it was women (or a woman) who first found the tomb empty at the resurrection, and according to Matthew and John it was to women (or to a woman) that Jesus first appeared after the resurrection. However we estimate these contradictory accounts of the first recipient of a post-resurrection appearance, it seems impossible to deny that women were among those to whom Jesus appeared after the resurrection.

When we turn to the witness of Paul, we cannot argue that Paul either refrained from ordaining women or prohibited their ordination because he did not know of the practice of ordination to ministerial office at all. If we are to answer fools according to their folly, we could point out that at Romans 16:7 Paul describes Andronicus and Junias as apostles, and that Junias could be a female name; if we accept the alternative reading of Julia in the very early (2nd or 3rd century) papyrus P46, she must be feminine. But we do encounter in an un-doubted letter of Paul one apparently serious difficulty in the way of ordaining women. He declares at 1 Corinthians 14:34–35:

> Let the women remain silent in the churches, for it is not permit-ted for them to speak; but let them be in subjection, as the law says. If they want to learn anything, let them ask their own husbands at home, for it is disgraceful for a woman to speak in church.

And two verses later Paul says that his hearers should know that 'what I write to you is the command of the Lord' (37), a remark which seems to apply to the whole of the preceding passage, not merely to the injunction prohibiting women from speaking in church.

Now if we are to take all Paul's commands and recommen-dations to his converts as automatically constituting immu-table laws of the church, all of equal weight to be converted directly into canon law, then indeed this passage offers a grave, indeed perhaps a fatal objection to the ordination of women. But to treat Paul's letters in this way is a most unwise practice,

112

which has been followed more than once in the history of the church, and has always resulted in confusion and disaster. Tertullian, especially in the strongly Montanist phase reflected in his later writings, attempted precisely such a task, and, hard though he tried, he could not help contradicting himself as well as falling into an absurd and unlovely legalism.

There are many passages where Paul enunciates lofty principles and imperishable truths, many where he gives sound advice of a practical sort useful in any age. But there are also places where he speaks simply like a Jew (or a Greek or Roman) of twenty centuries ago, living in a society made for men, run by men, where women were regarded as naturally inferior and subordinate. Not long before this passage, another in the same letter (11:2–16) states that women must keep their heads covered in church, using arguments so fantastic and obscure that nobody has been able to explain them satisfactorily. Are we to regard this trivial and ephemeral rule as constituting eternal sacred law? Obviously not. Then it must be admitted that not all Paul's injunctions are of equal weight and relevance and some were so much conditioned by their own time as to be wholly inapplicable today.

In another place (Colossians 3:11) Paul says that in Christ 'there is neither Greek nor Jew, circumcision nor uncircumcision, barbarian, Scythian, slave or freeman, but Christ is all and in all'. Are we to imagine that an equality which annihilates distinctions like this stops short at the distinction between men and women? No unprejudiced person reading the passage from 1 Corinthians 14 quoted above could fail to see in it the unreflecting, uncritical assumption of male dominance which was part of Paul's mind, rather than a command of the Lord. It is in the last degree unlikely that Jesus actually gave commandments about whether women should or should not speak in church.

The only other arguments against the ordination of women appear to be wholly *a priori* assumptions based on flimsy speculation, to the effect that God chose to be incarnate as a man and not as a woman and therefore could not desire that women should become priests. Very much the same argument could be applied against women becoming sovereigns or doctors or lawyers, with as much (or as little) force. In this area of

113

speculative fancy it is possible for two to play at the game: God chose to become incarnate through a woman, not (if we accept the story of the virgin birth) through a man. Therefore God wills that women, and not men, should be priests. But it is a waste of time to spend more ink on such trivial arguments.

Of very much the same type is the argument that there is something essentially male in the image of a priest. He is a father-figure and a woman cannot fulfil that role. But there have in fact in the history of religion been priestesses who have shown that they can fulfil certain priestly functions as well as men. And the examples of women like Mother Julian of Norwich and St. Teresa show that women could give spiritual counsel and command the respect of men in things spiritual quite as well as men even in ages when male dominance offered a far greater hindrance than it does today. The argument that there is something defiling about women handling sacraments and holy things can be treated only with the contempt that such superstition deserves.

The plain fact is that women do speak in churches today, in hundreds of churches all over the world, and that they do so with success. They speak, i.e. they preach and teach, quite as well as men when they are trained to do so. I have spent twentyfive years of my life teaching theology to women and can testify that they are just as intelligent as men and as capable of understanding and expounding theology. We live today in a society which is utterly different from the societies in which both Jesus and Paul lived at least in this respect, that women have become emancipated, are regarded as the equals (as well as the complements) of men, and have claimed for themselves and have been justly awarded entry into every other walk and profession in life, the law, the army, industry, medicine, the universities, politics, literature. Only certain parts of the Christian church forbid them to become priests. It is legitimate to wonder whether the leaders of those Christian communities who today continue to deny women access to the priesthood realize how ungenerous, how ignoble, how narrow and indeed how selfish they appear to those women who desire ordination and to those men and women who agree with them, and what a dreadful image of bigotry, timidity and conservatism the church, when it rejects ordination of

114

women, presents to the world.

There are women who are convinced that they have a calling from God to be ordained to the priesthood. The convictions of some may be mistaken, as may be the convictions of some men who desire the same. But we have no right to declare that their convictions must be mistaken, just because they are women. More than a hundred years ago George Eliot put into the mouth of Dinah Morris, the woman preacher in *Adam Bede*, these words on the subject:

> It isn't for men to make channels of God's Spirit, as they make channels for the water-courses, and say, 'Flow here, but flow not there'.

Ecumenical Priesthood

Finally it is worth pointing out that the doctrine of priesthood commended in this book offers opportunity for agreement about ministry between Christians of different traditions. I do not apologize for referring here to ecumenical relations, although in some theological circles to mention such a subject is to incur the charge of parochialism, or even obsolescence. Christian disunity remains a grave scandal and a serious hindrance to the true life of Christ's church and the true realization of Christianity. Theology gains no merit or lustre from deliberately ignoring the empirical church, no matter how apparently unexciting and unsuccessful that church may be.

The concept of priesthood expressed in non-cultic terms outlined in this book offers the possibility to those traditions which already preserve the priesthood, of recognizing in this sort of priesthood the true meaning and interpretation of their own, and to those traditions to whom the idea of a priesthood has hitherto been suspect or even anathema, it offers the chance of recognizing priestly elements in their own ministry uncorrupted by those traits and ideas which have hitherto repelled them in priesthood. It is not beyond the bounds of possibility that the Roman Catholic Church at least should recognize that the concept of priesthood expounded here is a permissible interpretation, that it has scripture and antiquity on its side, and even that it has possibilities of freedom and

115

flexibility which the medieval doctrine of priesthood could never have. There are some theologians in the Roman Catholic communion who are expressing dissatisfaction with the sacerdotal idea of priesthood on much the same grounds as those which this book has advanced, and who might be prepared to consider the alternative concept presented here.

On the other side, there must be very many ministers of religion in the Free Churches who do in fact—whatever they may be called—exercise a priestly ministry as it has been described in this book. There must be many—perhaps the majority—who stand for God to man and for man to God, and whose people recognize them as doing so, whether they express the ministry in these terms or not. There must be many Free Church ministers who struggle for their people, feel for them, pray for them, regard themselves as responsible for them before God, and also on the other hand speak for God to them, who have a conviction that they are commissioned by God in the church to minister to them a word, a revelation, a communication from God which cannot be simply identified as the wishes and ideas of the people themselves, but must in some way stand over against them, call them, even judge them. Such men (and women) are, in my view, already exercising a ministry which has a priestly character. Had such a concept been widely known and accepted when the recent scheme of reunion between the Anglicans and the Methodists in this country was being discussed, the issue might have been different. As it was, two extremes, one deluded by the vision of apostolic succession, the other following the will-o'-the-wisp of a scriptural ministry, united to wreck the scheme, while the majority in the middle were equipped with no clear doctrine of ministry to place against the convictions of those who opposed the reunion.

It is no coincidence that the doctrine of Christian priesthood set out in this book approximates more closely to the Anglican doctrine of priesthood than to any other. The intention of Anglicanism has always been to combine the proper elements of the Catholic and the Reformed traditions. It has not always succeeded. Sometimes it has only produced anarchy or unprofitable vagueness. But in its doctrine of priesthood I believe that it has successfully combined both Catholic and Reformed

116

traditions, and I set forth this conviction, not in order to crow in triumph over other denominations, but to offer to others as a firm ground for reconciliation between each other. This I believe to be the destiny in God's providence for the Anglican Communion.

SELECT BIBLIOGRAPHY

von Campenhausen, H. *Ecclesiastical Authority and Spiritual Power in the Church of the First Three Centuries*, London 1969

Couratin, A. H. 'Liturgy' in *The Pelican Guide to Modern Theology* 2, Harmondsworth 1969

Daniélou, J. *The Theology of Jewish Christianity*, London 1964

Ehrhardt, A. *The Apostolic Succession*, London 1953

Hanson, A. T. *The Pioneer Ministry*, London 1961

Hanson, R. P. C. 'The Church in Fifth-Century Gaul', *Journal of Ecclesiastical History* XXI (1) January 1970, 1–10

Groundwork for Unity, London 1971

'Eucharistic Offering in the Pre-Nicene Fathers', *Proceedings of the Royal Irish Academy* 76, 1976, C.4.75–95

'Amt/Amter/Amtverstandnis V', *Theologische Realenzyklopadie*, Lieferung IV, 1977, 533–52

Keresztes, P. 'The Jews, the Christians, and the Emperor Domitian', *Vigiliae Christianae* 27, 1973, 1–28

Leibrecht, W. (ed.) *Religion and Culture*, London 1958, 226–7, 234–5

Linton, O. *Das Problem der Urkirche in Neueren Forschung* 1932

Marrou, H. I. *A History of Education in Antiquity*, London 1956

Parker, T. M. 'Feudal Episcopacy' in *The Apostolic Ministry*, ed. K. E. Kirk, London 1946, 351–386

Riché, P. *Education et culture dans l'Occident barbare*, Paris 1962

INDICES

INDEX OF BIBLICAL REFERENCES

INDEX OF SUBJECTS

INDEX OF NAMES

127

Romans, the ancient, Roman Government, 24, 25, 31, 44, 62, 63, 69, 71, 73–74, 75
Rome, 12, 16, 39

Sadducees, 22, 23
Sceva, 31
Scotland, 86
Scythian, 113
Shakespeare, 7
Sicily, 76
Sidonius Apollinaris, 73, 74
Silvanus, 16
Society of Friends, 20, 110
Sodor and Man, bishop of, 87
Sohm, Rudolf, 18
Spain, 75
Stephen, bishop of Rome, 58
Stephen, 'deacon', 17
Symeon, 32
Synesius, bishop of Cyrene, 73
Syria, 45

Talleyrand, 78, 97
Teresa, St., 114
Tertullian, 21, 28, 29–30, 38–39, 40, 41, 44, 48–49, 50, 52, 54, 94, 113
Theoderic king, 75
Ticinum/Pavia, 74

Timothy, 12, 13, 16
Titus, 12, 13,
Tralles, 28

United States of America, 87
Ursacius, bishop, 72

Valens, bishop, 72
Vandals, 73, 74
Vatican Council, Second, 96
Vienna, Congress of, 97
Virgin Birth of Jesus, 22
Visigoths, 75
Vogt, J., 30

Wales, Church of, 86
Webster, dramatist, 7
Wesley, John, 87
Westminster Abbey, 77
William I, 77
Williams, Charles, 93
Willibrord, St., 77
Wilson, Thomas, bishop of Sodor and Man, 87
Winchester, 78
Wolsey, Cardinal, 103

York, 78

Zeus, 31